Cockatiels

Cockatiels

A Guide to Caring for Your Cockatiel

By Angela Davids

photographs by Carolyn McKeone

P R E S S

Irvine, California

Jerry G. Walls, *Editor-at-Large*
Honey Winters, *Design*
Indexed by Rachel Rice

The cockatiels in this book are referred to as *he* or *she* in alternating chapters unless their gender is apparent from the activity discussed.

Photographs copyright ©2006 Carolyn McKeone. Photographs on pages 97 (top), 99(bottom), 139, 156, 160, and 163 © 2006 Isabelle Francais. The cockatiel models in this book are courtesy of Cindy George; Shylo Adamson; Katarina Barton; Vickie Brundritt; Roberta French; Deb Giza; Kathy Killaire; Pet Paradise, London, Ontario; and Super Pet, London, Ontario.

The Library of Congress has cataloged an earlier printing as follows:

Davids, Angela.
  Cockatiels / by Angela Davids.
     p. cm.
  ISBN-10: 1-931993-71-8
  ISBN-13: 978-1-931993-71-5
  1. Cockatiel. I. Title.

  SF473.C6D38 2006
  636.6'8656—dc22

BowTie Press®
A Division of BowTie, Inc.
3 Burroughs
Irvine, California 92618

Printed and bound in Singapore
10 9 8 7 6 5 4 3

Acknowledgments

I WOULD LIKE TO OFFER MY SINCERE GRATITUDE TO cockatiel breeder and fellow author Diane Grindol for the expertise she willingly shared in the writing of this book. I would also like to thank Melissa Kauffman, editor of *Bird Talk* magazine and a personal friend and mentor for more than a decade, for providing insights into the pet owner's perspective. In addition, I'd like to thank Jerry Walls, experienced author and editor, for his groundwork and research, particularly on the topics of genetics and color variations. Finally, I'd like to thank my husband for being willing to listen to me talk about pet birds day in and day out.

—Angela Davids

For Cindy George, my wonderful bird wrangler and friend. Without her birds and help, these photographs would not have been created.

—Carolyn McKeone

Contents

1

The Charming Cockatiel

This group displays the special characteristics of the little parrots known as cockatiels. These slender birds have beautiful long tails and distinctive mobile crests.

Playful and affectionate, cockatiels are finding their way into more and more homes as adored pets. And they are the perfect parrot species for the first-time pet bird owner. Cockatiels are small parrots—bigger than budgies and lovebirds but about the size of the small conures—much smaller than African grey parrots and many other familiar pet birds. Cockatiels are generally easy to tame and not too costly to feed and cage (compared with larger parrots), and many cockatiels love to be handled and cuddled.

A Cockatiel Is a Parrot

Almost everyone can recognize parrots on sight. They have a distinctive appearance that includes feathers (of course!), a strong and sharply hooked beak, and feet that form an X, with two toes in front and two in back—a pattern known as zygodactylous. When parrots walk, their short legs give them a characteristic swaying motion. Most people also know that cockatoos and cockatiels have a crest whereas the other parrots usually don't, and most know that cockatiels are smaller than cockatoos. But that's probably about all the average person knows about parrots, cockatoos, and cockatiels. And that's probably all you've ever needed to know—until now!

Cockatiels Are Cockatoos

Parrots are a large family, or major group, of birds known as Psittacidae, and there are approximately 350 living species. They have no close relatives, although some ornithologists (scientists who study birds) have suggested relationships with such diverse birds as doves, cuckoos, and swifts. Parrots have a long fossil history and have even been linked to dinosaurs. Today, parrots are found around the world in the tropics and subtropics, with most species in tropical North and South America, in Australia, and in nearby islands such as New Guinea and Indonesia. Even the southeastern United States once had a widespread native parrot, the Carolina parakeet, which became extinct almost a century ago but was once found from New York to Texas.

Of these 350 types of parrots, just 21 species (give or take one or two, depending on which expert you consult) are properly called cockatoos. Many ornithologists now place cockatoos in a separate family called Cacatuidae, with cockatiels being members of the subfamily Nymphicinae. These birds range from pinkish Galahs to solid-black palm cockatoos. All cockatoos are found only in southern Asia and Australia, with more than half

This magnificent Eleonora cockatoo is showing off her large and impressive crest. She is heavier-bodied than your cockatiel, with a shorter tail.

the species found only on the continent of Australia; many species are restricted to a few small islands of Indonesia and the Philippines. Cockatiels are native to Australia, where they are widely distributed in the arid interior regions.

What Makes a Parrot a Cockatoo?

TO THE CASUAL OBSERVER, A COCKATOO IS A COCKATOO because she has a crest of erectile feathers on the crown of her head. The crest may be just a few feathers or many, long or short, and wide or narrow, but any cockatoo is likely to have a distinct crest. A few other parrots have crests, but these differ in structure (such as a few narrow, permanently erect feathers) or placement (such as being arrayed in a circle across the nape.) Cockatoos can also be identified by the lack of green feathers that are common in so many parrots. And—not that you can tell by looking—cockatoos have gall bladders, whereas other parrots don't.

But Isn't a Cockatiel Different?

Cockatiels certainly don't look like typical cockatoos. A cockatiel is slender, has a long and pointed tail, and has a small, delicate body. Cockatoos generally are heavier bodied and have relatively short and square or rounded tails. The cockatiel's color pattern also is very different. We'll examine the cockatiel in more detail later, but let's just say that under those pretty gray feathers a cockatiel is similar to a cockatoo in bone and muscle structure, the presence of a gall bladder and a specific arrangement of arteries coming from the heart, and the absence of any blue or green coloration in the feathers.

In the past, many owners and authors—and even a few scientists—considered cockatiels to be intermediate between true

Cockatiels often bond with each other as well as with their owners. These two don't even mind sharing a feed cup!

parrots and true cockatoos, but this is no longer the case. Studies of their genetic material show that cockatiels really are highly distinctive cockatoos, not relatives of other Australian parrots. Your cockatiel is just a modified cockatoo who has adapted to a specific way of flying and behaving, and over time she developed her long, pointed tail and unique coloration.

Fortunately for you, cockatiels differ from cockatoos in the very features that help make them excellent household pets. They are relatively small and have weaker beaks than most cockatoos do. Some can be taught to talk and whistle, but they do not produce the loud, frequent screams and cackles of some cockatoos. They can bond well with other cockatiels and with humans, have great personalities, and can breed easily in the home (although this is best left to experienced bird breeders). So you can easily understand why cockatiels are such popular pets!

The Cockatiel's Scientific Classification

Family: Psittacidae (all the parrots)
Subfamily: Cacatuidae (all the cockatoos)
Genus: Nymphicus
Species: Hollandicus
No subspecies are recognized—cockatiels are pretty uniform in structure, size, and coloration across Australia.
(Note: some ornithologists split off the cockatoos as a full family, Cacatuidae, in which case the cockatiel would form a subfamily, Nymphicinae.)

The Wild Cockatiel

A wild cockatiel is typically between twelve inches and almost fourteen inches long and weighs just three to four ounces, although selectively bred pets may be significantly larger. The birds have a wingspan of about fourteen inches or more, and the central tail feathers (which help make the cockatiel such a distinctive cockatoo) are six to seven inches long—about half the total length of the bird. This means that the body of a cockatiel is only about six inches long (not much longer than that of a budgie), making it the smallest of all the cockatoos.

Coloration is relatively simple and consistent, although it varies between the sexes. In both genders, the overall coloration is gray. Each wing has a large white patch that covers the wing coverts (the small feathers at the bend or "elbow" area) and the secondary feathers, so a resting cockatiel exhibits a wide white band along the outer edge of the wing. Females have a paler lower back area than males do; the outer tail feathers, lower

These gray pets (a female and a male) have the same color pattern as cockatiels in the wild do: gray overall with white wing patches, yellow heads (males), and bright orange ear patches.

back, and area around the vent, or cloaca (the common opening through which the feces, urine, sperm, and eggs all pass), are finely barred with gray and yellowish white; the undersides of the outer tail feathers are largely yellow; and the undersides of the wings are faintly barred. In males, the lower back and tops of the long central tail feathers are pale gray but uniform, and the undersides of the tail feathers are nearly black.

The head pattern gives cockatiels much of their charm and makes it easy to distinguish the males from the females. Both sexes have a large orange spot behind and slightly below the dark brown eye; this spot, often referred to as the ear patch, is on the feathers called ear coverts. The patch indicates the location of the ear opening, which is hidden under the feathers. The male's face is largely yellow, whereas the female's face, from the crown to the throat, is more gray than yellow. In males, most of the face patch is bright yellow, often becoming whitish toward the nape of the neck. The crest feathers (longer in front and usually curved to the front at their tips) are a brighter yellow in males than in females, who have mostly grayish crest feathers. In males, the orange ear patch is bright and well defined; in females it is often smaller, has indistinct edges, and is duller—at least in wild birds; selectively bred pet females may have faces and patches that are just as bright as the males'. In both genders, the back of the crown (behind the crest) and the neck are gray, as are the feet and beak. This color pattern is referred to as normal or normal gray.

The Cockatiel's Natural Habitat

Wild cockatiels are found only in Australia. They reside in dry locations in the interior of the continent rather than in more humid areas near the coasts. Flocks of cockatiels generally consist of ten to a hundred (although sometimes over a thousand) birds, and they are nomadic except during breeding season. They move rapidly from place to place in search of water and food and stay a few days or weeks until the resources are depleted. Some cockatiel populations are distinctly migratory, leaving the dry interiors and heading toward the wetter coast during the summer and during periods of drought.

Although large numbers of cockatiels can be found year-round in areas with a variety of plants and sufficient water, much of their territory could be called wastelands. Seldom true deserts, these are very dry savannas with sparse trees or bushes and patches of grass. Australian deserts may become virtually uninhabitable for breeding birds because there is no water for years at a time. Cockatiels also have adapted to living in the lap of luxury near suburban orchards and croplands, and they are perhaps most

Cockatiels and budgerigars—commonly called budgies—are often seen together in mixed flocks in the wild.

common on lands that have grass crops all year. Cockatiels may associate with budgerigars (also called budgies or parakeets) in mixed flocks, as the two species follow rain fronts and ripening grain crops across Australia. Both are extremely strong fliers who can cover long distances, and they have developed similar general shapes—and most notably, long tails.

Feeding in the Wild

Wild cockatiels are opportunistic feeders who eat a wide range of seeds and grains. Before the arrival of Europeans and their cultivated crops, the various wild grasses were probably the cockatiel's major food source. Today, however, cockatiels often feed heavily on fields of ripening wheat and millet; and although they will eat sunflower seeds, both ripening and fully ripe, they prefer smaller, drier seeds. When large flocks of cockatiels attack a field, they are considered crop pests and are shot, poisoned, or netted.

These babies and young cockatiels are perched just as they would be in the wilds of Australia. There they travel together in feeding flocks, seeking nourishing grasses.

In nature, cockatiels have a very predictable twice-daily feeding cycle. They feed first shortly after awakening, just after sunrise; unless they need to travel to look for more ripening seeds, the birds seek shade during the rest of the day. The second and major feeding period is about an hour and a half before the sun goes down. Cockatiels also drink twice a day at the same times they feed.

A Word on Budgies

COCKATIELS ARE CLOSELY ASSOCIATED WITH BUDGERIGARS in nature, and they are often found in mixed flocks. The two unrelated species have a similar shape and very long central tail feathers. The budgie (often called a parakeet) is a parrot whose scientific name is Melopsittacus undulatus. Budgies and cockatiels have very similar feeding and flocking habits and have adapted incredibly well to captivity, and today they are the two most common pet parrots.

Breeding in the Wild

Cockatiels spend most of the year in feeding flocks, but at the end of winter, pairs rejoin and begin to look for nesting sites. As do other parrots, cockatiels depend on rotting trees to provide nest holes, which limits their breeding range to areas with standing forests. Birds in the desert interior of Australia seldom breed there, instead moving toward coastal or mountain forests to breed and raise their young.

Cockatiel pair bonds are strong, and a pair may mate several years in a row. Pairs may also reuse the same nest hole if it is available. Most nest holes are located near water, where grasses

Cockatiels are wonderful parents, and they share parental duties. Unlike other parrots, cockatiel males and females both brood and feed their chicks.

are present. This makes the cockatiel's twice-daily drinking more convenient and ensures that some food will be available.

The female lays one to seven small whitish eggs, with a clutch of four being about average. The eggs are laid over several days, so there is always some disparity in development of the young in the nest. Both parents brood (sit on) the eggs, taking fairly regular turns for the roughly twenty days needed to hatch the eggs, and both parents feed the growing chicks, which is quite different from the behavior of most other parrots.

It is not uncommon for a pair of cockatiels to produce several clutches of eggs, either because the season is good (there is a lot of food and water) or to replace clutches that fail to develop or are eaten by predators. In bad years, survival of the young might be very limited, but in good years most of the chicks survive to fledge (leave the nest and begin learning to fly) in about five weeks. Fledglings may then remain with the parents for up to another month, learning to feed and fly on their own.

Then they leave the nest hole to join large feeding flocks of mostly young birds.

Cockatiels as Pets

Before cockatiels were introduced to America, they found their way to Europe. A damaged cockatiel skin was among the first bird specimens brought from Australia to England by Captain James Cook, somewhere around 1770. Later expeditions and then early settlers sent more specimens and eventually live birds back to Europe, where the cockatiels' unusual color and shape brought them quite a bit of attention. They proved to be good breeders even under the primitive conditions of European aviaries in the mid-1800s, and they were fairly popular in England and western Europe by the 1870s and 1880s. Writers of early parrot books admired cockatiels' antics and their abilities to speak and to imitate other birds, as well as how closely they bonded with their owners. There must have been a good number of birds in European aviaries by 1900 because the cockatiel became even more common as a pet after Australia banned all exports of cockatiels and other parrots in the 1890s. Cockatiels were kept and bred much as budgies were—another common pet and aviary bird at the turn of the twentieth century.

After World War I, several British authors published books on caring for and breeding cockatiels. By that time, cockatiels were also being kept as pets in the United States and Canada, probably having been brought home by returning soldiers and diplomats. Cockatiels were common and widely recognized little parrots in the 1930s, when large-scale breeding efforts brought down their price and made them even more widely available.

Many cockatiels love having their heads scratched. Your pet cockatiel can learn to sit on your finger to enjoy some one-on-one interaction.

Today, the cockatiel is ranked as the first or second most popular pet parrot, depending on the survey—virtually tied with the budgie. Cockatiels are found in tens of thousands in homes across North America, Europe, and Japan, and almost any pet store that sells birds has cockatiels for sale. Currently, normal gray cockatiels are reasonably priced, though commercially bred cockatiels of different color variations sell for double to three times the price of a normal. These color mutations (covered in more depth in chapter 8) are often bred to be shown in cockatiel exhibitions, and some of the rarer mutations may even sell for hundreds of dollars.

Probably at least a million cockatiels still live in the wilds of Australia, so the species is far from any danger of becoming threatened or extinct in the wild, even if the birds are treated as crop pests. Those bred in captivity represent the work of thousands of commercial and hobbyist breeders, as cockatiels breed equally well in large aviaries and in individual cages. Some hobbyist breeders have one or two pairs who produce half a dozen to a dozen young each year to give to friends or sell locally. Many in the pet bird community discourage home breeding by novices, though, because of safety concerns regarding the difficult care of cockatiel chicks and the possibility of overbreeding and producing unwanted birds.

Cockatiels spread oil from their preen glands over their feathers using their beaks.

2

Selecting a Great
Pet Cockatiel

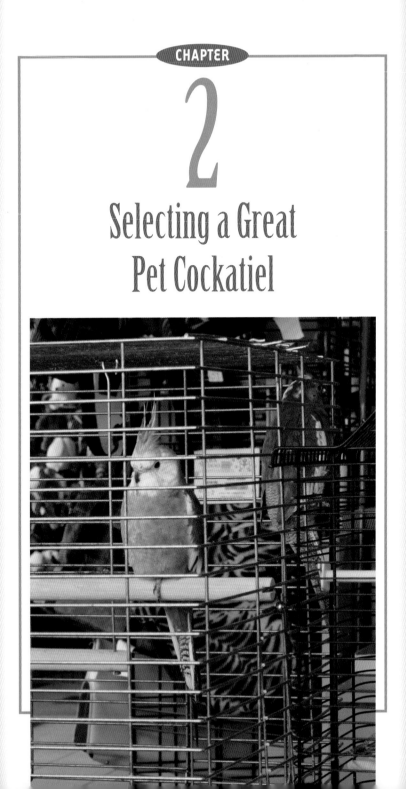

Buying your first cockatiel is an experience that the whole family can share. Take the time to visit many stores, breeders, and shelters to find the best pet for you.

COCKATIELS ARE WONDERFUL COMPANION BIRDS, AND they love to interact with their owners. They are affectionate and social, and they are always entertaining. And they are readily available. Almost any pet store that sells birds has a few cockatiels at most times of the year. It is easy to just walk into a store, look at the birds, and decide that you want a particular one. But this is never the way to buy a cockatiel—or any other pet. Before you rush out to buy your companion bird, take some time to make sure a cockatiel is the pet for you.

Will a Cockatiel Fit Your Lifestyle?

First, you have to seriously consider whether you can take on the responsibility of a cockatiel as a pet. Can you spend the time it takes to care for a cockatiel? You will be feeding the bird twice a day, checking his water and changing cage papers daily, and cleaning the cage more extensively every week. Birds are notoriously messy pets, so you can expect bird poop on the floor of the cage, on the perches, and probably outside the cage on occasion. Your bird will scatter food crumbs outside the cage and splash water all about as he happily bathes in his water dish. If you plan to keep a pristine house, then birds of any type are probably not the pets for you.

Are you willing to spend at least an hour, and preferably more, with your new pet every day, no matter how tired you are or if something comes up to take your attention away from the bird? Many cockatiels form close bonds with their owners, so you cannot plan to just put your bird in a cage in the corner, feed him, and otherwise ignore him. Cockatiels want company and must have attention to thrive. Buying a pair may reduce the amount of human interaction needed, but your pets (now both of them!) will still want your undivided attention for some time each day.

Is your house full of other pets? Some cockatiels get along well with budgies and with other small parrots, but they are not especially friendly toward finches and smaller birds (including canaries). Cockatiels are generally pacifists who get the worst end of the deal and could be hurt or traumatized by most other kinds of pet birds. Don't expect to just put mixed species of birds into one large cage to cut down on cleaning and feeding time. Cockatiels do best with other cockatiels, and even then you still may find two cockatiels who don't get along.

Some dogs have no interest in birds and simply ignore them, but other dogs may consider these pets to be either competition or toys. One bite from a dog can kill a cockatiel, and a

Your cockatiel will be happiest if you spend as much time as possible interacting with him. Set aside at least an hour a day just for the two of you.

playful swat with a paw can easily break a wing or a bird's back. Both cats and dogs should be supervised around birds, and they might need to be kept separate from the birds with barriers. Your cat may not go out of her way to attack a cockatiel, but certainly you cannot take your bird out of his cage if the cat can get into the same room. If you plan to let your cockatiel wander around a room, your cat will certainly look upon him as either prey or toy. Even a minor bite from a cat can cause infections that will kill a cockatiel, and a scratch from a cat's claw can be just as bad. Consider a cat scratch or bite as a veterinary emergency, and take your cockatiel in for life-saving antibiotics immediately. In short, consider any other animal in the household (including ferrets, guinea pigs, and reptiles) a potential danger, and closely super-vise their interaction—*if* you allow any interaction at all.

In addition to other animals, are there young children in your household? Children often love cockatiels, and these birds are certainly gentle enough to be safely handled by a child of perhaps twelve or older. However, cockatiels can bite and scratch, as any parrot might, and their bites can be quite painful. Their bones are delicate and easily broken, with often fatal results, and they react poorly to a handler's sudden moves. So for the safety of both, a cockatiel should not be left unattended with a child. If you take obvious precautions and teach everyone how to handle a bird, then a cockatiel can make an excellent family pet—family members can give the bird all the attention he desires.

Can you afford to maintain a cockatiel in the manner he deserves? Food is an ongoing cost, and you may find that the best varieties are quite expensive. Of course, because a cockatiel

Cockatiels make great companions for older children and adolescents, but they shouldn't be left alone with children younger than twelve.

Allergies

A **COCKATIEL CAN PUT A LOT OF SMALL PARTICLES OF** *many types into the air. Everything from seed hulls to powder from the feathers may circulate, not to mention a fine dust of dry bird feces, dust from the papers, and dust from the bird's pelleted diet. If you or anyone in your home has allergies, this could present a major problem. And dust from the cockatiel's feathers can also affect other birds in the house. If you think there might be a problem, check with an allergist to determine whether it is too risky to bring a cockatiel into your home.*

needs only a small amount of food each day, your costs are relatively low; but cockatiels are just as wasteful as any other birds and may throw out or ignore half the food you offer each day. Good cages are not cheap, and you will need to purchase a number of toys, perches, and treats to properly care for your bird. Two cockatiels may not be twice as expensive as a single bird, but don't expect the care of the second bird to be almost free. It's probably best to start out with only one bird.

What about veterinary bills? Your cockatiel will need at least a good basic examination when you purchase him and yearly checkups thereafter. (See chapter 6 for more on veterinary care.) If a problem shows up, you can expect more vet bills, and these can be quite high if special care is needed. Veterinarians are highly trained professionals, and they charge accordingly. Can you afford to budget a few hundred dollars a year for your cockatiel's veterinary care?

Are you prepared to have someone care for your cockatiel while you are away on vacation or business? Professional bird

Your cockatiel can be a messy eater and may waste much of the food you offer. He won't eat you out of house and home, but you'll have to pick up after him!

sitters are available in some areas, and it is best to have someone familiar with birds taking care of your pet while you are away. Your veterinarian may also provide boarding services—for a fee, of course. At the very least, you'll need to ask a friend or neighbor to check on your cockatiel daily, give him food and water, and tidy up the cage. Be sure to find someone who is happy to spend time interacting with your cockatiel so he doesn't feel too lonely while you are away.

Choosing the Color and Sex

When purchasing a cockatiel, color choice is purely personal. A cockatiel is a cockatiel, regardless of color; all color varieties of cockatiels bond with humans the same way and require the same

Noise Considerations

ALL PARROTS ARE NOISY, AND COCKATIELS ARE NO exception. *Fortunately, however, their small size means that their occasional screams and whistles do not carry far. But if you live in an apartment or town house and often keep your windows open, your neighbors will hear your cockatiel regularly. You may need to adjust your habits to be considerate of your neighbors.*

food, housing, and veterinary care. There are some slight differences between the sexes, however, especially in color, as detailed in chapter 1. When the first full plumage is in following the baby molt, you can distinguish the sexes of normal grays and many common color varieties.

A male cockatiel is very outgoing, often whistling and looking for a partner—bird or human. Many people prefer a male as a single pet because there is a chance he may talk. A female is

Though not as loud as larger parrots, cockatiels can be very vocal. Even if you don't mind the noise, you may need to make adjustments so your neighbors aren't bothered.

Many owners claim that females are sweeter, and that males are more likely to talk. If color is a factor, remember that normal gray males are a little brighter than females.

not as vocal as a male and will probably not learn to whistle or talk, although there are always exceptions. Both sexes exhibit sexual territoriality and aggression, but the females tend to be sweet birds. Another obvious difference is that females lay eggs, which may occur whether or not a male is present. Because it can be physically demanding for your cockatiel to lay eggs, it's best to prevent nesting behavior by keeping your bird to a schedule with only ten to twelve hours of daylight; more light encourages breeding behavior. (See chapter 7 for more on breeding and egg laying.)

If you want a single pet bird who might learn to talk, it might be best to choose a male over a female. Males are probably more colorful and are better singers, and they're certainly free of health problems related to laying eggs. It's also best to get a cockatiel who is weaned but not yet six months old; you'll have an easier time training a young bird.

Legal Restrictions

No one could possibly have anything against your keeping a cockatiel, could they? Actually, you might be surprised at how many apartment complexes and condominium communities have regulations that prohibit all or most pets. Many consider pets to be noisy, messy, or dangerous, and this could apply to your lovely cockatiel just as well as to someone's pet boa constrictor.

Actually, there might be good reasons to prohibit cockatiels in small apartments. They can be noisy birds, and some neighbors may not appreciate the noise. If not kept properly cleaned, the cage could become smelly and attract insects, pests, and other vermin. Of course, you will clean the cage daily and properly dispose of old papers and food, but the apartment owner and your neighbors may not know this. And many people just don't like animals. The lesson here is to check your lease carefully for any pet-exclusion clauses either before you move into an apartment or condo or before you purchase a cockatiel. Some cities and other communities place limits on how many pets you can have, even in a private home, and some have outlawed all exotic pets. Because all cockatiels are domestically bred and have not been exotic imports for a century, you wouldn't expect them to be legally defined as exotics, but this is not always the case. In some areas, exotic pets are defined as anything that is not a cat or dog; in others, the laws are so loosely written that any complaint against a bird is likely to cause you legal problems. Check with your local government about any such possible restrictions— they are rare, but you never know what the future may bring.

Because cockatiels are parrots, they may be suspected as carriers of psittacosis (once known as parrot fever but now more specifically called avian chlamydiosis by veterinarians), as well as illnesses such as Newcastle disease that can harm flocks of domestic chickens. Some areas have outlawed ownership of all parrots as a simple way to prevent any disease problems, but such broad bans seldom apply for long. (See chapter 6 for more on common bird diseases.)

Because all cockatiels are bred in captivity and the species is still abundant in Australia, your pet does not fall under any Convention on International Trade in Endangered Species (CITES) regulations about importation of birds from foreign countries. However, there are restrictions on carrying pet birds across state lines in some states (especially California and Hawaii) and across the borders from the United States to Canada and Mexico. Quarantine periods at special federally run or state-run facilities may be required (for a fee), or special health permits guaranteeing that a cockatiel is free of contagious diseases may need to accompany the bird. It is probably not a good idea to simply try to carry your pet across state lines without consulting your veterinarian and researching the regulations of the states involved. Moving pet birds across international borders is usually very complicated and sometimes impossible.

All Pet Stores Are Not Equal

When selecting a pet cockatiel, consider it just as important to check the "health" of the pet store as to determine the health of the bird. Judge each shop individually. Ask questions of the management and employees, and ask to look behind the scenes if possible to see how birds are fed and handled. (Young cockatiels get their first taste of human bonding in the pet store.) Ask about the ages of the birds sold, about warranties offered by the store,

This pet store has a large selection of birds, cages, and accessories. Shop around for a clean, well-kept facility. Other sources for pet cockatiels are breeders and shelters.

and what happens if your bird should suddenly become seriously ill or die within a week or a month. The store, regardless of size, must be clean. You can't expect a bird cage to be spotless, of course, but at least the droppings should be fresh, normally formed, and not covering birds in the cage. Food should be abundant and fresh. There must be no obviously sick birds in the store; bird diseases can spread quickly from a parrot of any type to other parrots, or even to parrots from finches. Many states and cities require that pet stores not only be licensed but also pass regular health inspections; ask to see licenses and other permits if you have any doubts about the store. Cleanliness, a written health guarantee, recommendations from bird owners or a bird club, and willingness to help you are always positive signs about a store.

Keep in mind that a pet store isn't the only source for finding your pet. Reputable breeders also have healthy birds. Again, fellow pet bird owners and bird clubs are excellent sources for recommendations. When you visit a breeder's home or aviary, look for cleanliness, toys in the cages, healthy food, and plenty of room in the cages for the birds to exercise. Ask your breeder about his or her experience, and confirm that he or she will be available to answer any questions you have once you take your bird home.

Pet birds are sometimes available for adoption from animal shelters or through bird rescue groups. See the appendix at the back of the book for a list of parrot rescue organizations.

Assessing General Health

There are physical signs you can observe in a cockatiel to assess his general health. If you don't have any experience with birds, bring along a friend who has birds, or try to find someone from a local bird club to tag along to show you what to look for. You can't expect to find everything that a veterinarian will notice, but certainly there are some simple observations you can make to eliminate some unhealthy birds—or become fairly confident that the cockatiels being sold in a specific pet store are in excellent health.

What to Look For

A cockatiel's eyes should be clear and bright, never dull, sunken, or covered with an opaque or mucous film. The eyes should be a deep, dark brown (virtually black) in both young birds and adults, although some color varieties have red eyes. The beak should be well formed and symmetrical; it shouldn't be bent to one side, obviously overgrown at the tips (in older birds), or have very irregular edges that seem to be flaking off. If you give the cockatiel a fresh seed, he should be able to hull it without any problem—he should be able to use his tongue to work the seed

Make Sure Your Cockatiel Is Weaned

JUST BECAUSE A COCKATIEL IS OFFERED FOR SALE *doesn't necessarily mean that he is ready for you to take home. The best aviaries and breeders produce good birds from healthy parents and fully wean them onto an adult diet. Less scrupulous breeders turn out marginally healthy birds who are passed on to pet stores as soon as the cockatiels become recognizably feathered. These birds may still be dependent on their parents for feeding.*

Unless you have a lot of experience hand-feeding cockatiels and have lots of spare time, never buy a cockatiel who is not fully weaned. You can often distinguish unweaned birds by their behavior: they cry persistently and may bob their heads when you are near, begging to be fed. Ask the pet store if the bird is fully weaned before you buy him. Better yet, place a deposit on the bird and then pick him up two or three weeks later, making sure that he is still healthy by having a veterinarian give him a checkup within a few days of bringing him home.

against the beveling on the inside of the beak to remove the hull. If you suspect that the tongue is damaged (because the bird can't handle a seed), move on.

The bird should be able to balance himself comfortably on a perch, and he should be able to use his wings and legs to mount and dismount quickly. A cockatiel walking across a cage floor may appear to be struggling because of his waddling gait, but this is normal. Make sure that the toes are all present, as are the nails, and that the toes open and close normally. Look for bumps on the legs and toes that could indicate unclean conditions in the

A healthy bird like this one has bright eyes and a well-shaped beak. He should be alert, and his feathers should lie flat.

cage and minor infections. And ask the bird's age; it's extremely difficult to tell the age of an adult bird. Mature birds have longer crests than juveniles do, but you can't tell whether an adult is two years old or fifteen.

Be sure that the feathers are fully and correctly formed. Do they lie flat and in the correct directions? Young cockatiels often have incomplete feathering under the throat. In some color varieties, especially the lutino, birds may have a bald spot behind the crest, but this is never desirable. Are the feathers around the vent clean, with no signs of diarrhea? Although most cases of diarrhea are simply reactions to changes in foods, some can indicate serious or even deadly diseases. Be sure to check the cage bottom for signs of diarrhea or loose droppings of any sort. Look for droppings that are bright yellow or lime green—both may indicate serious diseases. (But also know that the color of the droppings is strongly influenced by the color of the foods being eaten.)

The flight muscles, those on either side of the breast, must be strong and solid. They are a good indication of proper health. If there is obvious excess fat under the skin (which may appear as badly placed feathers, or the chest may appear "bosomy"), the bird may be obese; if so, a veterinarian can recommend a new or modified diet.

The cockatiel must have a good personality. Don't buy a bird who bites or backs into a corner and sways, hisses, or chal-

Don't overlook the feet when assessing a bird's health. This is an example of healthy feet, able to grip the perch and showing no irregularities.

This lutino shows a lot of personality! You want your pet to be active and playful, interested in the world around him and ready to bond with you.

lenges you with beak and nails. Such a bird may not have been handled enough when very young or may have been mistreated; you want a bird you can handle every day. The best birds are the ones who come up to you and actually want to be touched, even while still in a cage with other birds. If the breeder and the pet store have done their jobs correctly, the cockatiels offered for sale are hand tamed and allow gentle handling; it's an added bonus if they already know to hop onto a perch or your finger when you touch their feet or chest. Almost any cockatiel will bite if stressed or surprised, so give the bird a chance to notice you, and talk to the bird before placing your hand in the cage. Biting must never be the normal reaction to a hand coming into the cage.

At the same time, beware of birds who don't react to your presence. A normal cockatiel is alert and active (unless it's time to sleep, of course) and is curious about intrusions into his space. If a bird just sits on the perch with his head on his breast or his wings drooped, suspect that he is ill, not just exceptionally tame.

Parrot illnesses can spread very rapidly, so it is never a good idea to take pity on and try to nurse back to health an obviously ill cockatiel; you won't succeed, and you might spread the disease to other birds in your home.

A Vet Visit

It is important to take your bird to a veterinarian who specializes in pet birds within the first couple of days, even as soon as the day of purchase. This is not just a good idea for the health of the bird; a veterinary exam is often required by pet stores that offer written health guarantees. Health guarantees typically state that the bird being sold is believed to be in good health, and if a veterinarian discovers an illness within a specified number of days, then the store will replace the bird. More important, your bird deserves a medical examination. Because they are prey species, birds do not readily show that they are ill; to display signs of illness would mark them as easy targets for their natural predators. A veterinarian will be able to perform lab tests that will give true indications of your bird's health.

The first exam (discussed in detail in chapter 6) gives a diagnostic baseline that the veterinarian can use to quickly help diagnose illnesses or abnormal conditions that develop later. As all animals do, cockatiels develop various natural conditions as they grow older—everything from respiratory infections and yeast infections to molting problems and gout—and these are easier to detect if the veterinarian has the bird's medical history. Your bird's weight is also a good indicator of his health, so having it on record makes the weight easy to track.

When considering a cockatiel for purchase, add another two hundred to four hundred dollars over the base price. This should cover most aspects of a general exam and baseline lab work. It's the price of peace of mind and the first step in protecting your new bird's health and longevity.

The Final Choice

It is your responsibility to choose a good cockatiel—not the veterinarian's, not the pet store's, and not the breeder's or animal shelter's (or any friend or relative who might have offered you a bird). The pet store should offer you a good selection of healthy birds, and the veterinarian should assure you that the bird you have selected is healthy, but the final decision is yours. Choose a color and sex you find appealing. Look for the best bird you can afford—one you can be sure you will enjoy for the next ten to twenty years or more!

Don't be shocked if you see that your bird is losing feathers. Cockatiels molt about twice a year.

This is a healthy and alert pied-colored cockatiel. (See chapter 8 for details on color variations.)

3

Cockatiel
Housing and Care

In addition to needing loving attention and a good diet, your cockatiel needs a comfortable home and a wide variety of toys to chew on, climb on, and explore.

BECAUSE THE EMPHASIS OF THIS BOOK IS ON KEEPING just one or two cockatiels as household pets, there won't be much discussion of flight cages and aviaries, which are large, costly structures designed to house groups of birds outdoors. You can easily keep a couple of cockatiels in the average home or apartment without going to great expense or building your own cages.

Rule One: Be Prepared

There is one important rule for housing cockatiels: buy the cage and basic supplies before you buy a cockatiel! This means that when you start looking around at cockatiels in different shops, you should also be looking at and comparing different cages. See what sizes, what materials, and what designs are available. Some cages are better designed for cockatiels than other cages are, and some designs just won't work for parrots of any type.

At least one day before you are ready to pick up your new pet, buy the largest cage you can afford that has the appropriate bar spacing for a cockatiel. The bars should be from half an inch to three-fourths of an inch apart to be sure the cockatiel can't get her head stuck between them. In the wild, cockatiels are ground feeders, so your pet will prefer a wide cage in which she can waddle about, rather than a tall one she can climb. The cage may already include food and water cups, but buy at least two extras for use when the main cups are being washed. Ask a pet store employee to help you select appropriate-size perches of various diameters, several safe toys, and a supply of the food the cockatiel you are purchasing is currently eating.

Bring everything home, set up the cage on a table or proper base (which is often included with higher quality cages), and make sure that everything fits where you want it. Be sure to leave room for your cockatiel to stretch her wings and roam about the cage, and don't place perches above the food and water cups (to keep them free from droppings). When you bring your pet home,

Don't Forget Rule One!

NEVER BRING HOME A COCKATIEL FIRST AND THEN LOOK for a cage! Your new pet will not enjoy remaining in a small cardboard carrying box or even a larger travel cage while you prepare her cage; she wants to look out at the world and make herself at home as soon as she arrives. You don't want your life with your new pet to start with a sulky, moody, frightened, and uncomfortable bird.

This cage is perfectly placed in a well-lit room that gets plenty of traffic. Your pet will appreciate being "part of the action" and will benefit from the stimulation and interaction.

place her in the new cage and leave her unhandled for at least a day while she gets used to her new home. Talk to her to make her feel welcome, but leave her undisturbed in her cage.

Where to Put the Cage

Before you buy the cage, decide where you will put it and how you will make sure it is stable. A cockatiel wants human companionship as much as possible, so her cage should be placed where you two can interact throughout the day, not just for the mandatory hour of "hands-on" time. Not all of your interaction with a cockatiel needs to be physical; she will derive pleasure from watching you and interacting with you verbally.

Put the cage in a bright, comfortably warm, draft-free area located away from noisy activities; your cockatiel may try to compete with the noises she hears. If the cage is near a TV, remember that you won't be able to watch past your cockatiel's bedtime! The cage also shouldn't be near a door, as this can be drafty; the same applies to an often-open window and to air conditioning and heating ducts. Avoid dark closets and unused bedrooms, as a bird tucked into an obscure place receives little attention and never bonds properly. The cockatiel is part of your family, and you should stay in contact as much as possible, speaking to her and petting her each time you pass by.

A cockatiel needs to know that the sun is rising in the morning and setting in the evening so her body rhythms coordinate with changes of days and seasons. She does not need access to direct sunlight, and direct sunlight could quickly overheat both your cockatiel and the cage. Never place the bird near a

Kitchen Caution

KEEP COCKATIELS OUT OF THE KITCHEN. IT MAY SEEM TO be a good place for the bird, as the kitchen often is a busy, friendly place, but there are just too many dangers in a kitchen: stoves, sinks, garbage disposals, nonstick cookware (the fumes can be toxic to birds), hot water, knives, toxic foods—you name it. The dangers are just too great, even if you are vigilant.

window that receives full and direct afternoon (western) sunlight, as that may be too warm; a few hours of morning (eastern) sunlight is fine and helps parrots metabolize vitamin D.

A Stable Home

Some cages have hooks at the top so the cage can be hung from the ceiling or from a special stand. This may be fine for canaries and finches, but cockatiels are active birds who feed mostly on the ground and therefore need more stability. A hanging cage is easily set swinging by any movement inside or outside the cage, which disturbs the bird and may even cause her to stop eating. Your cockatiel's cage should come with its own stand, and good-quality cages have sturdy ones. If not, put the cage on a stable piece of furniture such as a table or bureau. The cage should be at your chest level or higher because cockatiels don't like to be looked down upon.

Like any pet birds, cockatiels can be messy, so most good cages have "aprons," or food catchers, around the bottom to reduce the spread of debris. This is always a good feature to look for in a cage. If you place your cockatiel's cage on a table designated strictly for that use, you can put similar edging strips around the table. And if there is space for a playgym (which cockatiels love), you'll have a complete cockatiel habitat!

Cage Size and Type

Cockatiels like exercise; they seldom become "perch potatoes" unless forced to exist in a small cage without an opportunity to exercise outside the cage. Try to buy the largest cage (within reason) that you can afford. For a single cockatiel, the cage should be no less than roughly two feet square and thirty inches high. A cockatiel can spread her wings to about fourteen inches, and it would be ideal if you could give her a cage about double her wingspan in width. Two cockatiels can be kept together in a cage only minimally larger than this, but of course they would prefer having more room. A cage about three feet long and wide and thirty inches high would be quite satisfactory for either one or two cockatiels.

Large parrots can bite through many small bars, but cockatiels are not destructive birds and don't need especially heavy bars on their cages. The best type is stainless steel, although affordable and attractive anodized aluminum and powder-coated cages are now becoming widely available. Look for bars held together by crimps rather than spot welds; welds are made with a lead compound that may be toxic to birds when chewed. Welds also commonly loosen with time, exposing the rough ends of the bars, which can injure your bird. Avoid cages made of wood or acrylic. Your cockatiel might pick at any weak spots in the wood and eventually chew through it; and the wood or the paint on it may be toxic. Acrylic travel cages are fine for housing your bird temporarily, but they often don't provide enough ventilation for everyday use and don't have bars on which your cockatiel can climb and get exercise. Cages made of both metal bars and acrylic are an option; they do provide sufficient ventilation and climbing opportunities, and they also help contain the mess.

Cage Design

The fewer the frills in a cage, the easier it is to clean—and the more space available for the bird. Check that the door or doors are large enough to let you easily reach all corners of the cage for cleaning—and so your bird won't crumple her tail feathers when

The bars on this cage are perfect for cockatiels: they're spaced three-fourths of an inch apart and offer opportunities for climbing. The "penthouse" playgym offers extra exercise and stimulation outside the confines of the cage.

Toxic Materials

BEWARE OF CAGES MADE OF TOXIC MATERIALS. SOME (usually cheap) cages are made from galvanized wire, which is iron wire coated with a zinc compound. Even when properly soaked and brushed to remove excess zinc, galvanized wire poses a danger: if your cockatiel chews it, she can suffer from heavy metal toxicity, which could kill her. Other cages have bars coated with plastic or rubber to improve the appearance and often to cover shoddy construction. Cockatiels and other parrots love to sit and pick at wire coverings, but plastic and rubber are toxic to birds, creating dangerous compounds in the stomach or forming obstructions in the gut. Chromed wire and accessories also are potentially toxic, as the chromium coating often begins to peel off over time and can be chewed by a cockatiel; chromium is a heavy metal and toxic when eaten.

entering and leaving the cage. Take a close look at the door's locking system as well. Cockatiels are relatively intelligent parrots and can often figure out simple sliding latches reachable from inside the cage. The latch should be bird proof yet not so complicated that it takes a mechanical genius to get into the cage.

Although cockatiels spend a lot of time on the floor of the cage foraging for dropped food, they also like to climb the sides of the cage. This means that a cage with almost all vertical bars won't work well; leave those for canaries and finches. Cockatiels and other parrots need several horizontal bars on each side of the cage to give them climbing exercise. (And they also need time for exercise outside the cage.)

The floor of most cages is either a pullout tray alone or is made of the same bars as the rest of the cage with a pullout tray that sits beneath it. The tray should be positioned in the cage so the cockatiel cannot reach its edges and chew on them. Because cockatiels spend much of the day walking around on the floor, the floor must be stable, heavy, and easy to clean. You can line the floor of the cage or the cage tray with black-and-white newspaper (color may be toxic), paper towels, cage paper made for bird cages, or a nontoxic cage litter manufactured specifically for birds.

Cups

Most quality cockatiel cages have cups for holding food and water. If your cockatiel frequently dirties her water, you might want to switch to a water bottle (usually attached to the outside of the cage). At first, supply both a water bottle and a supplemental water cup. Cockatiels are curious and quickly figure out how to drink from a bottle, but be sure your bird has the hang of it before removing the water cup.

Most quality cages come equipped with perches and cups, but it doesn't hurt to have some extras on hand to use as substitutes while you're cleaning the others.

Perches

A cockatiel needs several good perches—preferably at least three or more perches per cage at different heights and angles. Cockatiels like to jump or glide from one perch to another, so pairs of perches are often preferred. Perches are made of many materials these days, and because they might be chewed regularly, they should be easily replaceable. They must be stable, fitting securely between the bars of the cage, and they should be about half an inch in diameter, whether round or oval. The best perches vary somewhat in diameter along their length so all cockatiels can find a comfortable position as they stand. Grapevine and manzanita branches that have been sandblasted to remove the outer bark (and any possible parasites and pathogens) make great perches because they are so varied in size; just make sure that the pieces you buy can attach easily and securely to the cage bars.

Don't choose perches that are covered with sandpaper or other abrasive surfaces designed—in theory—to provide a continuous manicure for the cockatiel's nails. The nails should be kept under control by regular inspection and trimming, not by a passive sheet of sandpaper. A very rough perch will eventually damage the cockatiel's feet, causing small cuts and abrasions that can become infected and produce a condition called bumblefoot. Perches made of concrete are available and are fine as long as you use only one concrete perch at any given time.

Be prepared to clean the perches every few days. The simplest routine is to buy several extra perches and place clean ones in the cage while you are cleaning the dirty ones. Scrape the perches with wire brushes (there are semicircular brushes made especially for perches) to remove loose droppings, soak them in a

These cockatiels look quite at home on this natural perch. Although the branch is large in diameter, the wood is has bumps and ridges, offering a variety of footholds.

bleach-and-water mixture or a bird-safe cleanser (available at pet stores and from veterinarians), and then rinse and dry them. Never allow feces to accumulate on a perch; this will almost ensure that your bird's feet will become infected. Make sure perches are not located above food and water cups, where the cups can become contaminated by droppings. And never place one perch above another if you have two cockatiels in a cage; you know what will happen!

Bath Time

Not all cockatiels like water, but those who love to splash in shallow water get totally wet and then dry their feathers in the sun, as they would in nature. If given a bathing cup for a few minutes every two or three days, a cockatiel will make a true mess but enjoy every minute of it. It may be less messy to use a fine mist from a plant misting bottle to occasionally soak a bird, although it may not be as fun. Whichever method you choose, make sure the water is tepid, never hot or cold. After a bath, the cockatiel will use her beak to take oil from the preen gland at the upper base of her tail and smooth it onto her feathers to groom them.

At Night

A COCKATIEL MUST HAVE HER SLEEP! TYPICALLY SHE stays in a better mood and is healthier if given about twelve to fourteen hours of light, activity, and companionship and about ten to twelve hours of darkness and quiet, although these are not hard and fast numbers. This is why the cage should not be located near a TV that is on late at night. Cockatiels go to bed early and will learn to get up with you in the morning. The simplest way to make sure they get enough sleep is to move the cage into a quiet, dark room at a specific time each night, perhaps eight o'clock. Just be sure the room does not become too warm or cool, and leave a night-light on if the room is very dark. (When startled, cockatiels can be prone to night frights, discussed later in the chapter.) You also can use a cage cover—a thick fabric hood—but cover only three-fourths of the cage so some light is visible.

Special Lights

Cockatiels are diurnal, which means they are active during the day. In nature, entire flocks retire to protected areas in trees as the sun goes down, and the birds don't budge until the sun rises. Cockatiels also come from notoriously sunny areas and are used to being exposed to considerable sunlight during the day. Sunlight is important for converting chemicals in the skin and blood into vitamins and enzymes, and sunlight helps ensure that calcium and other minerals metabolize properly. Unfortunately, the chemically active wavelengths of sunlight are mostly in the ultraviolet (UV) range, and UV light is largely blocked by ordinary window glass. So even if a cockatiel's cage is placed in morning sunlight each day, the cage may not receive enough UV light—and it may get too much heat. You may want to take your pet and her cage outdoors—such as on a screened porch or on a deck or patio—for a few hours each week. (But never leave her unsupervised!)

Cockatiels have been bred in captivity for more than a century, and they have shown little need for direct sunlight. However, some people believe that their birds do better, have better attitudes, and breed better if given access to special UV lights, or full-spectrum lights, for at least an hour a day. These lights, similar to those used by basking lizards and turtles, are made to mount in special fittings above the cage and can be outfitted with a timer to turn on and off each day at designated times. Take special caution to keep them out of the bird's reach to prevent burns and shocks. Do you need special lighting for a cockatiel? Probably not. But, if you have the money and interest, it wouldn't hurt.

Travel Cages

Consider purchasing a suitable travel cage for your new pet when you buy the bird. The bird's home cage will be too large to fit easily into your vehicle and may not be sturdy enough for travel. You will need a good cage for travel to the veterinarian at least once each year, so plan ahead. The cage doesn't need to be elaborate, just large enough for your cockatiel to travel comfortably.

Travel cages needn't be fancy and shouldn't be very large—just big enough for your cockatiel to sit comfortably and small enough to fit in your vehicle.

Toys

All parrots need toys to keep themselves amused, and cockatiels are no exception. If forced to stay in a cage with nothing to do, a cockatiel soon becomes morose or hyperactive, and her health disintegrates; she may pluck or pick at her feathers or chew on her toes or the cage wires, and she may become a screamer or biter. Purchase at least three toys to start with, and rotate them with one or two other toys each week as you remove them for cleaning.

Any pet store should have cockatiel toys for sale, and most of these toys are fine if they do no more than give the bird some-

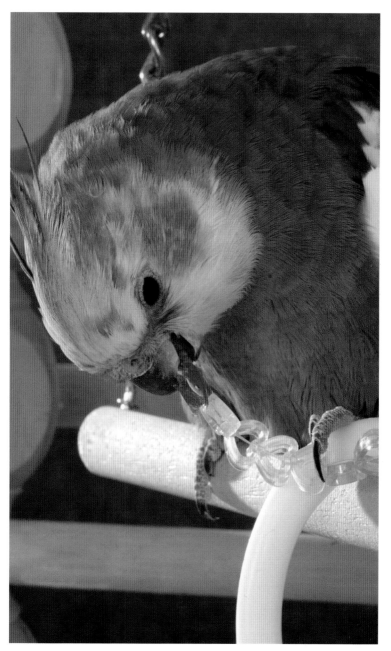

When choosing toys, be sure that none contain toxic materials, and check your cockatiel's existing toys periodically for any damage that might do your bird harm.

thing to hang on, climb, pull on, or chew on. Just make sure that they are safe toys. Avoid anything with rubber that the bird could chew, and look for stainless steel fittings—not zinc-loaded galvanized metal—in chains and hanging hooks. If rope is used in the toy, make sure it is not so unraveled that the cockatiel could get a nail caught in it. And any coloring must be nontoxic.

There are a lot of different types of cockatiel toys available, and some are especially designed for preening or chewing. Cockatiels like the sound of small bells and really do enjoy looking at the strange bird in the mirror. Glass mirrors could break and cause cuts, so most toys use plastic mirrors. Strips of rawhide and untreated leather also make good toys and will keep a cockatiel busy for long periods, as will small blocks of wood. Don't wash these toys when you wash out the cage; you'll need to discard these items when they become old or soiled. Cockatiels also like toys on the floor of their cages, though these might be difficult to keep clean. Toys need not be expensive, but you have to be sure to check them regularly and replace or repair any showing wear. Often, you can salvage part of one toy and combine it with parts from another toy. Be creative, but make sure the toy is safe.

Playgyms

Playgyms (sometimes called playstands) are the ultimate accessory to keep a cockatiel busy and healthy. Playgyms may be simple, with just a few wooden bars or branches, or very elaborate and incorporate a variety of ladders, swings, and perches. Playgyms are designed to be used outside the cage, often on an adjacent tabletop or on top of the cage where the bird can be allowed some freedom for a few hours or more each day—always

Simple or complex, a playgym is a wonderful accessory for a cockatiel, offering plenty of opportunities for exercise outside the cage.

under supervision, of course. Playgyms give the cockatiel plenty of room to spread her wings and hop around, chew on the perches or branches, climb ladders, play with a variety of hanging toys, and generally have fun. Some playgyms use pieces of manzanita and grape vine, and others use acrylic rods and perches. Elaborate playgyms can be quite expensive, so you may want to start with a basic model and add additional toys, swings, and ladders later as your budget allows.

Outdoor Cages

Few average bird owners have outdoor cages for their cockatiels, but you may want to build or buy a sturdy, safe cage that allows your cockatiel to be outdoors a few hours a day during good weather. Many companies now make affordable small flight cages (although still expensive compared with the usual indoor cage) that are easy to set up and maintain. The problem with an outdoor cage is that the bird is subject to sudden changes in weather, predators, accidents, and even contamination from diseases spread by wild birds who fly over her cage. It really is difficult to be sure your cockatiel is safe when she is outdoors, even if you are around all the time, as you should be.

Cockatiels can enjoy a surprising range of weather conditions, and they are quite tolerant of temperatures as low as fifty degrees Fahrenheit (even lower if given time to adapt) and as high as the low nineties as long as shade is available. Cockatiels like having hiding places and do not like direct sunlight, drafts, or cold rains. If you decide to allow your cockatiel outdoors, either in a cage or loose on your shoulder while wearing a bird leash (see the section "Allowing Free Flight"), just be very careful. You'd hate to lose your friend.

Routine Care

Cockatiels are birds of habit, and they like a regular schedule. Give them fresh food and water each morning. Check that toys are in good condition and that perches are clean. Feed the birds again near sunset, which corresponds to their natural feeding cycle. And put them to bed by roughly eight o'clock so they can get plenty of sleep.

Try to handle your pet for at least an hour each day, preferably about the same time (or times, if you have multiple handling sessions). This helps sustain the bond between the two of you and keeps the bird happy. Of course, it doesn't hurt if you handle your pet more each day—generally, the more the merrier. Use the time for petting and cuddling, and also spend some time trying to teach her simple tricks. Your cockatiel will enjoy every minute of attention, but if you see that she is getting tired and touchy, let her go back into her cage and relax. A few cockatiels never really enjoy handling, but these are exceptions.

Once a month you will have to check the nails and if necessary trim them, and probably twice a year you will have to trim the wing feathers. These activities are best learned from your veterinarian or an experienced pet bird owner or breeder, because if done incorrectly you could harm your pet. Both grooming tasks are discussed in detail in chapter 6.

Cage Cleaning

In addition to the day-to-day care of your cockatiel, much of your time will be spent making sure the cage and all accessories stay clean. Perches should be cleaned at least every two days, and the entire cage should be cleaned weekly. Movable items should be soaked in a 10-percent chlorine bleach solution (or a bird-safe cleaner recommended by a pet store or veterinarian) for at least fifteen minutes, then thoroughly rinsed and dried before being returned to the cage; no chlorine or cleaner smell should remain. All litter or paper in the bottom of the cage should be removed regularly and replaced. Never let old droppings accumulate in a cage. Not only is it unsanitary, but it also makes cleaning more difficult and time intensive.

Allowing Free Flight

A surprising number of cockatiel owners allow their birds to fly freely (or almost freely) around their homes—under supervision, of course. Free flight can be dangerous: cockatiels can fly into mirrors or windows, get into trouble in the kitchen, chew on electrical cords, disappear into the dirty laundry, become prey to cats and dogs, or fly away through an accidentally opened door or window. At the same time, free flight does permit a cockatiel to get a lot of exercise and stay close to humans. You may want to allow your bird to move around in a single room that has been carefully checked to remove any dangers. An hour or two a day of such freedom can improve a cockatiel's mood tremendously without reducing her bonding to the owner.

Before allowing any free flight, make sure that your cockatiel is perch trained. (See chapter 5.) This means that if you

This pair is enjoying free roam of the room—but supervised, of course. They're on the floor now, having safely fluttered down on trimmed wings.

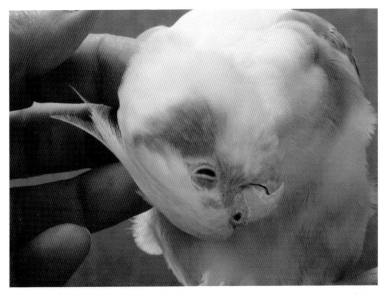

It's hard to tell from this photograph, but this cockatiel is showing pleasure at being scratched by grinding her beak.

gently present her with a perch, she will climb on and allow you to retrieve her. This helps prevent problems if the bird should decide to park herself in a high corner or on a light fixture—or even escape outdoors into a tree. Cockatiels are very strong fliers and can't be safely taken outside unless in a cage or perhaps on a bird leash, even if the bird has trimmed wing feathers. (Wing trimming is discussed in detail in chapter 6.)

Common (and Odd!) Behaviors

If this is your first experience with a cockatiel, you may be puzzled by some of her actions. Cockatiels do have some unique behaviors that you won't see in other pets. When they are relaxed and content, cockatiels often grind their beaks—a sure sign that they are happy. The placement of the crest also indicates the mood: a relaxed adult holds the crest down (young birds

These two cockatiels are using their crests to communicate. The one on the left is alert, and the one on the right is relaxed.

often hold it erect the majority of the time), a startled bird holds the crest straight up, and an angry cockatiel holds the crest back. A male in particular may show dominance on occasion, lifting his wings up high over his head to make him appear bigger. Although this behavior is generally directed toward another bird, cockatiels may show dominance to you if they are defending their cages.

Like most parrots, cockatiels are preeners: they spread oil from a gland at the base of their tail over their feathers. Preening not only makes cockatiels look shiny but also helps waterproof their feathers. Cockatiels also molt: about twice a year, cockatiels

You'll probably observe your cockatiel grooming her feathers by preening, and if you have more than one bird, they may groom each other.

lose their feathers, which are replaced with new ones. It's a gradual process, so your bird is never completely bald, but the feather loss can be startling if you aren't expecting it.

Night thrashing (or night frights) is another common behavior among cockatiels, although the reason for thrashing is not clear; perhaps it's because cockatiels can't see well in the dark and feel unprotected. Even bumping into a toy in the cage can trigger thrashing. You can try to prevent night frights by keeping a night-light on in the room. If you awake to hear your cockatiel thrashing about, turn on the light and speak softly to calm her down; then check to make sure she hasn't suffered harm.

This wing flapping says, "I'm bigger than you are!"

Your cockatiel is sure to be an entertaining and affectionate pet.

Feeding
Your Cockatiel

Your cockatiel's diet will consist mainly of pellets, but some variety is always welcome. Start with the diet your pet was fed in the store, and gradually introduce new foods.

Some parrots are difficult to feed, requiring specific diets and defined percentages of various types of foods. One of the reasons cockatiels have become popular as pets is because their diet is not so complicated; they could actually survive for a limited number of years on a diet of small mixed seeds. If you want a really healthy and long-lived pet, however, you will certainly need to give your bird more than just seeds day in and day out.

The Beak Tells All

In nature, cockatiels are not specialized feeders. They eat a wide variety of seeds from many different plants—grasses through trees—and at various stages of maturity, from immature, soft

This cockatiel is thoroughly enjoying munching on a millet spray.

seeds to older, hard seeds. Because cockatiels feed mostly on the ground, their preferred foods are likely grass seeds of various types, including grasses from the dry inlands of Australia (also a favorite natural food of budgies). However, cockatiels in the wild have also adapted to feeding on ripening grain crops such as wheat and grain sorghum.

The beak tells the story of how a cockatiel (and other parrots) feeds. The upper beak is longer than the lower and overlaps it, ending in a relatively sharp point. The lower beak is blunt and wide across the tip, which fits into steplike grooves in the upper beak. The cockatiel uses the tip of the upper beak to pry seeds out of grass heads and manipulate them into the mouth. Once the seed is in the mouth, the tongue—which is very specialized in parrots—holds the seed in place and rolls it against ridges inside the lower beak while both beaks apply significant force against the seed. At some point, the hull (outer coat) of the seed cracks; then the tongue rolls the seed so the hull peels away,

The Gut

THE COCKATIEL HAS A RATHER COMPLICATED DIGESTIVE system designed to predigest seeds before they reach the actual stomach. From the esophagus, or gullet, the hulled seed goes into a large crop. At the lower end of the crop is a short, muscular tube (the proventriculus), somewhat equivalent to the stomach of a mammal. This leads to the larger, much more muscular ventriculus: the back stomach, or gizzard. In some birds, the ventriculus is lined with heavy, hard spines and tubercles that grind tough seeds and finish digestion, but because cockatiels hull seeds before swallowing them, the ventriculus is relatively weak. The intestines of a cockatiel are fairly short and end at the cloaca (or vent). Like other birds, cockatiels technically do not have an anus because products aside from digestive waste—such as sperm and eggs—enter and leave the body through the common opening, the cloaca.

and the kernel of the seed (the soft, nutritious part) is swallowed. The hull is then spit out, the next seed is picked up, and the process starts over. Each seed is individually hulled and swallowed; there is no chewing and no gulping down of meals. It's entertaining to watch your cockatiel eat seeds in this manner, but your pet needs more than just seeds.

Pelleted Diets

Today, many pet cockatiels are raised on pelleted diets, which are nutritionally balanced diets. Each pellet has all the proteins, carbohydrates, fats, vitamins, and minerals required, eliminating the need for additional vitamins. Pelleted diets come in a great variety of sizes, shapes, and colors, and many mixtures are manufactured specifically for cockatiels. If your

Offer your cockatiel a varied diet of pellets (85 to 90 percent) and seeds and treats (10 to 15 percent).

bird was not weaned onto a pelleted diet, he might take a while to decide which color or size he prefers; expect some waste for the first several weeks when you present the new food. Eventually, however, cockatiels will adapt to a pelleted diet, although they almost always prefer seeds.

Seeds Are Still Good

Pellets constitute a balanced diet, but you can still provide seeds at each meal—about 50 percent of the total offered at first if your bird has been on a seed-only diet—and then gradually reduce the amount of seed over two to four weeks.

Veterinarians recommend a diet that is 85 to 90 percent pellets and 10 to 15 percent seed and other treats (which can include healthy human foods like vegetables and pasta). Ask your veterinarian about the proper proportions for your individual birds, based on their current weights and general health. It is true that cockatiels live well on just pellets, but they seem to enjoy seeds as a form of entertainment. Some pellet manufacturers have begun including a healthful ratio of seeds in the same packages as their pelleted diets, providing just the right amount of fat and a bit of fun.

Cockatiels like seeds that are small and not especially hard. The seeds they prefer are easy to hull, and most have a high fat content. However, it is possible to give too many fatty seeds and make your bird overweight. For this reason, mixtures of seeds are preferred over a steady diet of just one type. Generally, seeds can be broken into two groups: those low in fats and those high in fats. Both types should be present in any diet.

This is a basic cockatiel seed mix with some hulled and unhulled sunflower seeds added to the mix for variety.

Low-Fat Seeds

Low-fat seeds are high in carbohydrates and relatively high in protein. The three most common starch seeds average about 55 to 65 percent carbohydrate, 10 to 15 percent protein, and 4 to 10 percent fat. They are also good sources of calcium and other minerals.

- Canary Seed: This small, pale brown seed is widely available and often forms the basis of seed mixes sold for small birds, from finches to budgies and cockatiels. Your pet will quickly hull each seed individually, so blow away the empty hulls regularly to see if any whole seeds are there.
- Oats: Oats are sold both as whole seeds and as groats, which are hulled seeds. Oat groats are often used as fillers in seed mixes, but they are not a bad food. Oats (especially groats) are easily digested.
- Millets: There are many species and varieties of millets sold, but all are rather hard, round seeds. Various types of millet are available in heads or sprays that you can hang over a perch or clip to the side of the cage. Because millets are low in fat, they are often considered a great base seed in mixes.

High-Fat Seeds

High-fat seeds, which may be quite large, are excellent for growing birds and ill birds, but they contain too much fat to be used as more than a small percentage of the entire mix. These seeds may consist of more than 40 percent fat, with a lot of protein and very few carbohydrates. Fatty seeds are often fed during the winter, when they provide quick metabolic heat, and they are fed only in small quantities during the summer.

- Niger (nyjer): It's hard to believe that such small seeds could have much nutritional value, but each seed contains roughly 40 percent fat, 20 percent protein, and over 10 percent carbohydrate. Niger becomes rancid quickly when exposed to humidity and heat, so it does not store well.

- Safflower Seed: This bitter seed has perhaps the best mix of fat (30 percent), protein (15 percent), and carbohydrate (30 percent) of all the common seeds, but for some reason few birds like it. Therefore, is not a major part of a cockatiel seed diet.

- Sunflower Seed: Sunflower seeds are easily produced in your garden, forming by the dozens in the black centers of the flower. (Hanging a ripening flower head in the cage can produce some very excited cockatiels!) The ripe seed is covered with a hard oval hull that varies from mostly white with black stripes to solid black (oil sunflower). The hulls are hard to break, but the heart is sweet and full of oil (about 45 percent fat and 25 percent protein). Cockatiels can hull sunflower seeds, but they prefer to eat them the easy way—as hulled sunflower hearts or the sunflower chips found in many seed mixes.

Unfortunately, a diet heavy in sunflower seeds is certain to cause obesity, and hulled seeds and chips spoil rapidly if not kept in a very dry container. Sick cockatiels can digest sunflower hearts quickly and well, so they are a good additive to the diet of an ill bird.

None of these common seeds is native to Australia, but this makes no difference to cockatiels. Good mixes usually consist of about half canary or white millet, with the other half red millet, oat groats, niger, and sunflower chips or hearts. Summer diets should contain starchier seeds, whereas winter diets usually have more sunflower hearts and other fatty seeds.

Sprouting Seeds

Sprouting seeds contain higher levels of some vitamins than the seeds themselves do. Soak the seeds in a little water for about twenty-four hours; then rinse them in lukewarm water, and place them on a plate. Cover the seeds so they don't dry out; they should sprout in about forty-eight hours. Rinse them again and let them dry before offering them to your bird. Be sure to remove any uneaten sprouts after a few hours, as harmful bacteria can grow on any wet food.

Fruits and Veggies

Although a cockatiel will live well on a combination of pellets and seeds, most cockatiels like the occasional treat of some greens. Most fruits are very high in sugar, but there is no harm in giving small bits of apple or banana a few times a week. Many cockatiels enjoy yams or sweet potatoes, spinach (in moderation), defrosted frozen peas, zucchini, winter squash, parsley, and carrots.

Your cockatiel might also enjoy a small leaf of green lettuce, kale, or spinach or even some small broccoli florets, which serve as a natural source of moisture and provide many vitamins and

When giving your cockatiel fruits and vegetables, make sure no pieces are larger than your thumbnail. One grape to a cockatiel is the equivalent of forty to a person!

Some cockatiels may be picky about their vegetables just as many people are. Some prefer cooked veggies, whereas others will eat only raw ones.

minerals as well. You can hang them from the top of a cage on a special hook available at pet stores or just clamp them in place with a wooden clothespin. Some cockatiels will eat small slices of red bell peppers—an excellent source of carotene that will enhance the bird's yellow and orange coloration.

People Food

Your cockatiel will want to eat what you eat; he's a member of the family, after all. However, most human foods are not good for parrots and can't be digested. Some exceptions you could offer are a one-inch slice of corn on the cob (hold the butter!), a few green beans, or a spoonful of well-cooked noodles or rice without sauce. Do not feed your pet bird any fatty foods or spicy or salty foods, and never offer chocolate or avocado, which can be toxic. Cheese can be very difficult to digest, so avoid offering that as well.

Animal Products

Many cockatiels occasionally grab a moth or beetle that happens to find its way into the cage. The birds can use the protein and seem to have no problem digesting small insects. In fact, there is some evidence that insects may form a significant portion of the wild cockatiel's regular diet during nesting season, and insects are fed to the growing chicks as a source of extra protein. Putting a few crickets or small mealworms in the cage once a month does no harm and could give your cockatiel some needed exercise.

Avoid milk products. Parrots do not have the enzymes to allow them to digest milk, and it can lead to bad cases of diarrhea. A cuttlebone or mineral block is a much safer source of extra calcium. However, an ill bird who is recovering from treatment with antibiotics may be given small amounts of yogurt

Grit

containing live bacterial cultures. This helps replace good bacteria in the gut that were killed by the antibiotics. Mixtures of these bacteria (*Lactobacillus acidophilus*) are available in many pet stores.

Cockatiels do not need meat in their diets, but giving boiled egg to breeding cockatiels is standard practice. The egg must be thoroughly cooked and then grated or sliced very thinly and added to the food. Because egg spoils very quickly, it cannot be left out for more than a few hours. Some breeders feed dried egg powder to breeding females who are developing eggs.

Foods to Avoid

If you occasionally add treats to your cockatiel's diet, take care not to give him something that could be poisonous. Avoid offering salted foods and those with butter or other oils, for the same reasons you limit them in your own diet. Unsweetened chocolate (and milk chocolate, to a lesser extent) contains high levels of theobromine, which can cause an irregular heartbeat and death; avoid all chocolate to be safe. Many garden flowers are toxic to humans and mammals, and it is likely that some might be dangerous for cockatiels as well. Sunflowers are fine (as you might expect), and so are flowers from apple trees, roses and rose hips, and nasturtiums, but it is best to avoid feeding your bird all other flowers and wild greens.

Vitamin Warning

BECAUSE PELLETS ALREADY CONTAIN ALL THE VITAMINS your bird needs, it is not necessary to add vitamin drops to the food. In fact, if you were to add supplements of vitamins A, D, or E to the recommended diet (of 15 percent seeds and other treats and 85 percent pellets), you could easily produce an overdose—called hypervitaminosis—which could harm your pet. If the basis of your bird's diet is seeds, sprouted seeds, or a rice and bean mash, then you need to add vitamins to the diet. Check with your veterinarian to learn the right dosages and how best to give these vitamin supplements.

The pit of the avocado contains persin, a very toxic compound that sometimes leaches into the surrounding flesh of the fruit. Even small amounts of persin can kill a bird as small as a cockatiel, so it is best to avoid avocado in any form—including guacamole. The pits of peaches and cherries contain toxins, so if you offer these fruits (even in dried form), be sure no traces of the pit are present.

Make Changes Gradually

When you buy your cockatiel, feed him the diet he is used to, and pay close attention to what he is eating and what he is wasting. For the first few weeks, stick to the same diet. Cockatiels will eventually try many different foods and may learn to love them, but they are slow to recognize new items as food. If you want to change your cockatiel's current diet, alter it gradually, allowing several weeks for the bird to get used to the new food. Add the new food in small amounts at first, and expect it to be ignored or thrown out. Eventually your pet will accept the new diet, and he may actually come to prefer it.

Everyone enjoys a treat now and then, and your cockatiel is no exception. This bird may be getting a treat as a reward or just out of love.

5

Training Your Cockatiel

This well-behaved cockatiel is quietly sitting on a perch outside her cage. Training is important not only for ease of handling but also for peace of mind. If she flies to a high spot in the house, you can retrieve a trained bird by offering her a long perch.

It's natural for cockatiel owners to want to show off their birds' talents to family and friends. Although many people are satisfied with having a pretty bird that is healthy and responds well to handling and petting (a great goal), others want their birds to perform tricks or learn to speak. Although cockatiels are quite intelligent, they may not learn tricks easily and may never speak. But they are not difficult to tame, and they adapt well to handling.

Bonding: Start Early

Training of any type is always easiest with a young bird and is often not possible (beyond the basics) with an older bird. The problem is that cockatiels (and other parrots) typically bond at a very young age either to people or to other parrots. If fledgling cockatiels are removed from their siblings and weaned by hand, they soon learn to associate handling by a person with food and pleasure. If kept separated from other cockatiels and always treated gently and as members of the family—with a lot of interaction time—they will remain tame and train easily and might learn to speak or whistle. This is why breeders and pet stores charge higher prices for hand-fed cockatiels.

If young cockatiels are left with their clutchmates, fed by their parents, and then put into a cage with other cockatiels, they will bond with their cockatiel relatives. But that doesn't mean they can't be tamed or won't make good pets. Much depends on the temperament of the individual cockatiel, as some hand-raised birds simply don't like people, and some parent-reared cockatiels love human attention. When choosing a cockatiel, look for one who likes you, who is comfortable with you, and whom you believe you can work with. Then learn to accept what you can do with your particular cockatiel, rather than

Petting Your Pet

EVEN AN UNTRAINED COCKATIEL CAN LEARN TO ENJOY petting and being fussed over. Many older birds learn to come out of their cages (on their own) just to sit in someone's lap and have their heads scratched. If you don't try to hold them tightly and only gently stroke the area behind their crests, they will stay calm. Keep in mind that many birds are territorial and may not appreciate your hand in the cage. If yours is territorial, simply open the cage door and let your cockatiel come out to you; then offer your finger as a perch.

comparing your bird with someone else's or with an ideal of what you think a pet cockatiel should be.

If possible, get a hand-fed cockatiel, who should train quickly. She will transfer the bond with her previous handler to you and be eager to please you. If you can't get a hand-fed bird, buy the youngest fully weaned cockatiel you can find, and house her separately (even out of hearing range) from other cockatiels. You have to form a bond with her first and then start training, but the two processes follow naturally.

One simple way to get the bird used to you is to offer her treats. Given the right goodies, a cockatiel will do almost anything within reason. The best treats are bits of millet spray, a favorite color of pelleted food, or even a sunflower seed. Cockatiels all have different tastes, so experiment a bit.

When you get your bird, place her in a fully furnished cage with familiar food in her food cup. As mentioned in chapter 2,

Both owner and bird are enjoying a moment of bonding. A hand-fed cockatiel will bond to you quickly and be ready for training right away.

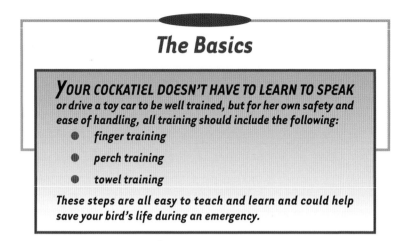

The Basics

YOUR COCKATIEL DOESN'T HAVE TO LEARN TO SPEAK
or drive a toy car to be well trained, but for her own safety and
ease of handling, all training should include the following:

- **finger training**

- **perch training**

- **towel training**

These steps are all easy to teach and learn and could help
save your bird's life during an emergency.

leave her there for a day so she gets used to the cage and the
different sounds in the new environment. After a day, prepare to
start your basic training, and start giving her as much attention
as possible, even when she's not being trained. Choose a short,
simple name (one or two syllables), and say it each time you go
near the cage. Talk to your bird each time you go in to change
the food and water or to clean the cage. Talk slowly and in an
even tone, which inspires confidence.

Finger Training

Basic training usually starts with teaching the bird to hop onto
either your finger or a small perch while she's in her cage. Put your
hand into the cage with the index finger extended, and leave it
there—motionless—for several minutes. Most cockatiels will
become curious and walk over to your hand. After two or three
repetitions, the bird should consider walking onto your hand and
finger. At this time, start using a single-word command, such as
up, whenever the bird approaches. Eventually the bird will associate hopping onto your finger with the command.

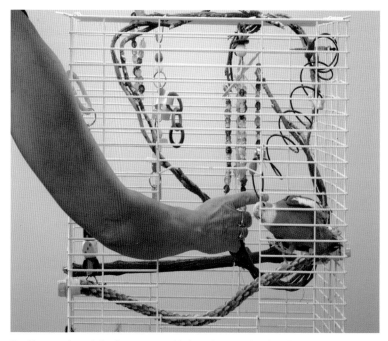

The first step in training is to get your bird used to your hand in the cage. If your pet is territorial, let her come out on her own and then approach her.

Let the bird take her time learning this first step. Never try to corner your cockatiel and force her to hop onto your finger, which will only scare her. If the bird starts screaming and trying to escape, don't back off completely; stay near the cage, and offer gentle words of encouragement. If the bird tries to bite, move your hand away from the bird but only just out of reach. You can stay there for a minute or so and try again, or you can continue the training session after the bird has come out of the cage on her own. You may also want to do your training in a "neutral" territory, such as on a playgym, to reduce the chance of territorial biting. If your bird is still nippy, a final option is to begin *up* training with a perch (discussed later in the chapter) and work up to using your finger.

Keep your training efforts to roughly ten-minute intervals, spaced about an hour apart at first; then extend them to fifteen minutes and increase the frequency. Offering a treat during training may help your cockatiel learn that your hand is not harmful.

Once your bird hops onto your finger (or palm) on command, the next step is to slowly withdraw your hand from the cage with your bird on it. This may frighten her at first, so keep your movements slow and steady. Your cockatiel's natural curiosity about the world outside her cage should quickly get the best of her, and she will learn to move around while on your hand. If she flutters to escape, return her to the cage at first. If she escapes into the room, carefully and patiently catch her and return her to your finger to be placed back into the cage. This step may take quite a while for some birds to learn, but almost any cockatiel will get used to standing outside the cage on your finger or hand.

Next, teach your bird to get off your hand on command. Slowly return her to her cage; then, with a simple command such as *down* or *off*, tip your finger forward (and possibly shake it gently) to encourage your bird to step down onto the cage floor or onto a perch inside the cage. Repeat the up and down lessons over a period of days until you are sure your bird understands the commands and will respond when outside the cage. Practicing the commands will come naturally to you both as you interact with your bird each day. Her curiosity should lead her to explore other potential "perches" on your body, such as your shoulders or the top of your head.

Remember that any trip outside the cage can be dangerous. Be sure that the room in which you train is safe—check electrical outlets and cords, remove possible high perching spots, and don't let in any other pets. And remember that it is never safe to take

This bird has learned the first lesson—to step up onto a finger from a perch.

Patience

even the best-trained cockatiel outdoors on your hand or shoulder without a leash. Cockatiels are nervous birds who startle easily.

Perch Training

At some stage during training, try to substitute a simple perch (half an inch in diameter works well) for your finger. Some birds respond better to a nonliving perch than to a finger, which might scare them. Perch training is important for your bird's safety as well. If your cockatiel should ever escape to a high spot in a room or even a tree, there will be no safe way to get her down unless she is perch trained.

Slightly roughen the training perch so your bird can get a good grip with her nails, or purchase a textured perch for your training sessions. At first, try a perch about a foot in length, moving to a perch four or five feet long as you teach your cockatiel to get down from a high spot.

A finger-trained bird should already have a strong tendency to step off your finger on the *down* command, so start there. Gently

Lesson two accomplished: stepping down from a finger or perch to a perch or to the cage bottom.

This cockatiel is stepping from a finger to the perch, but not all birds are comfortable stepping onto fingers. Using a perch is a good alternative.

place the perch against your cockatiel's belly, and move the perch down toward the feet. Give the *down* command, and your bird should move from your finger to the perch. Teach her to move from within the cage to the perch on the *up* command as she would to your finger. You may need to repeat this lesson many times, but teach your bird to move from any spot to the perch on command. It's a simple trick, but a very useful one.

Towel Training

Some cockatiels object to being handled by a stranger, such as a veterinarian, and they fight it beak and nail. An injured bird also resents being handled and may even bite her owner when approached. Many breeders train young birds to accept being wrapped in a towel just for these reasons; ask the breeder or pet store employee whether your new bird has already been towel trained. If not, you might want to teach your cockatiel yourself.

Take advantage of your bird's natural interest in toys and treats. Place a favorite toy or a small treat such as a bit of millet spray in the center of a towel, and let your bird get used to playing or taking a treat there. After a few repetitions, slowly raise one corner of the towel over the bird. After she gets used to this, move to two corners, then three, and so on until she tolerates or even enjoys being inside the towel. Remember to make this a play period as well as a training period. You want your bird to enjoy it, so include friendly and playful talking and petting as part of the training. You want the experience to be pleasant for her.

Talking

Wild and untrained cockatiels are natural mutterers and whistlers. Males whistle long and loud when trying to get your attention or

Although she appears to have something to say about it, this cockatiel has learned to accept being wrapped in a towel for easy handling at the vet's office.

the attention of another bird. Females are less vocal than males, as a rule, and will probably not learn how to talk or whistle.

Training to Talk

Start with a young male cockatiel who is well bonded to you and preferably has been finger and perch trained. House him separately from other cockatiels or parrots and in an area where he cannot hear the radio or TV. You want him to be able to concentrate on your voice and just your voice. Placing a cockatiel being taught to speak with other cockatiels is generally a waste of time, as the natural instincts and sounds will win over the strange sounds you are trying to teach him.

Start with a simple word, such as *hello* or the bird's name. In a quiet atmosphere and preferably with the bird on your hand, distinctly repeat the word with a slow, constant cadence until he

What to Expect

NOT ALL COCKATIELS WILL LEARN TO REPEAT WORDS OR
phrases, but a few can develop a vocabulary of a few words.
Because of the bird's small size (and small sound box), your
cockatiel's voice will always sound high-pitched and even
screechy, although it should be easily understood with experience. You can never expect to hold a conversation with cockatiels, but they can understand things that are important to
them, such as the names of foods and treats; the words bath,
good-night, hello, and good-bye; and the names of people and
other pets in the household. (Dr. Irene Pepperberg has done
more than twenty-five years of research showing that parrots
can understand the words they say. For more information on
parrot intelligence, go to http://www.alexfoundation.org.)

loses interest—generally, about ten minutes. Return the bird to
his cage for a break for fifteen or twenty minutes, and then take
him out and start repeating the word again. Do this several times
a day until the bird takes the hint and starts trying to repeat the
word. Be patient; it may take quite a while before your cockatiel
learns the first word.

Once the first word is learned, move on to the second word
using the same routine, reinforcing the first word learned as well.
You might find the bird enjoys repeating his name so much that
it is hard to turn him off, but eventually the second word will
join the first as part of his vocabulary. The first words usually take
considerable time to learn, but often the next few take much less
time and effort. Stick to very simple words, preferably one- or
two-syllable words that contain a hard sound and are easy to say.

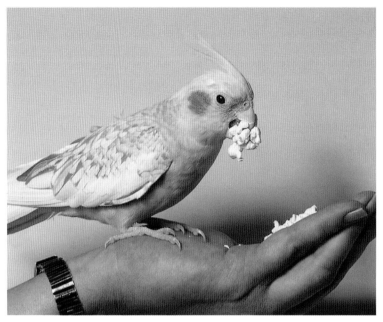

No matter what behavior you're trying to reinforce, a treat is a great reward for a job well done—and an incentive for repeating the behavior!

Even if this cockatiel never learns to drive a truck, he can enjoy playing with it!

Talking Aids

Repetition is the key to teaching a cockatiel to speak, and it may take a large part of your day to do it correctly. For this reason, tapes, CDs, and even DVDs that contain a basic vocabulary for all speaking parrots are now widely available and popular. The recordings consist of a speaker slowly repeating several selected words—seemingly forever. These media are most effective if you listen to them with your bird, repeat the word yourself, and also use the word at times that the media is not playing. In the end, the social interaction between you and your bird is the crucial factor in teaching him to talk.

Bad Company

You can certainly keep untrained cockatiels together, but it is wise to separate trained and untrained birds once training begins. A speaking cockatiel will learn to screech if placed with screeching untrained birds, and a trained bird may forget how to step onto your finger if the other birds in the cage are afraid of your hand. You have the greatest chance of success in training your cockatiel if she is the only cockatiel in your household and you spend the time with her.

Of course, there are exceptions to this isolation rule. When a trained cockatiel is housed with another trained bird, each re-inforces the other's training to some extent—one may actually teach the other a new trick. Sometimes talking cockatiels teach all their cockatiel friends to talk!

Contrary to what you might think, it is possible to breed trained cockatiels. They have natural instincts to fiercely protect their young during breeding, but they will be just as tame or trained once they have finished rearing their babies. This is a special characteristic of cockatiels that isn't shared by most parrots.

TEACH YOUR COCKATIEL TO TALK

Saying the same word over and over can get tiring, to say the least. Try some of the training recordings on the market, to reinforce the words you're trying to teach.

Even if your bird never learns tricks and never masters the art of talking, you'll still have a fun and loving pet.

6

Keeping Your Cockatiel Healthy

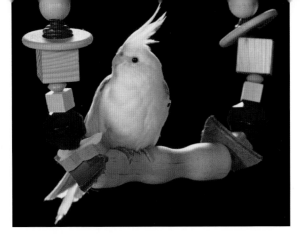

Your cockatiel may be your companion for ten to twenty years. Keep him in good health by offering a nutritious diet, toys and exercise, regular visits to the veterinarian, and plenty of love and attention from you.

COCKATIELS ARE VERY HARDY BIRDS, BUT THEY ARE subject to a variety of bacterial and viral illnesses, some of which are highly contagious from bird to bird. Cockatiels can develop deficiencies if kept on a nutritionally poor seed-only diet. And if cockatiels are fed too much and not exercised, they become overweight and unhealthy. Although you can regulate your bird's diet and try to protect him from illness or harm, it's important to develop a close relationship with a veterinarian who specializes in, or is very familiar with, parrots.

Finding a Veterinarian

When you buy any pet, you have a moral obligation to take him to a veterinarian for regular checkups. Many veterinarians have

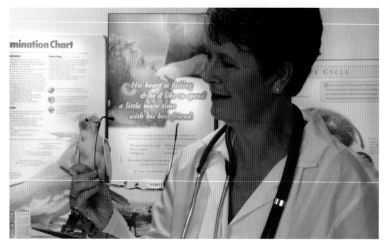

Not all veterinarians are knowledgeable about bird care. Look for a veterinarian who is certified in avian practice by the American Board of Veterinary Practitioners (ABVP).

some experience with birds, but you should try to find one who is certified in avian practice by the American Board of Veterinary Practitioners (ABVP). These veterinarians have the title Diplomate ABVP—Avian Practice after their names, or they are described as board-certified avian veterinarians. You can locate one of these highly qualified avian veterinarians by calling the ABVP at 800-697-3583 or using the search tool on the ABVP Web site: go to http://www.abvp.com/finddiplomate.aspx and enter your city and state.

Because the requirements for ABVP certification are so demanding, there are only about one hundred veterinarians certified in avian practice, so it may be difficult to find one in your area. An alternative is to select a member of the Association of Avian Veterinarians (AAV). Membership in this organization is a strong indicator of both a veterinarian's experience with birds and his or her interest in staying up to date on avian medicine. There are currently about three thousand members of the AAV

Quarantine

WHEN PARROTS ARE IMPORTED INTO THE UNITED *States, they require a period of quarantine to see whether any latent diseases appear that can be treated. Cockatiels in local pet stores are seldom—if ever—imported, but they often do pass across state borders. Import laws vary widely from state to state. Some states require a veterinary health certificate or a minimal quarantine period to observe the birds for symptoms of diseases. If your bird was brought in from another state, there may be legal paperwork that should accompany him at the time of sale. Before you buy a cockatiel, ask whether he was bred locally or came from a breeder in another state.*

worldwide, and they can be located through the AAV Web site at http://www.aav.org. Enter your city, state, zip code, or area code into the search tool at http://aav.org/vet-lookup, or call 817-428-7900.

Don't be afraid to ask veterinarians questions about their educational backgrounds and professional experience. Good veterinarians may be hard to stop once they start talking about the good old days at school and how much they love caring for pet birds.

The First Examination

Your cockatiel's recorded medical history starts with the first checkup by a veterinarian. Parrots have an elevated metabolism compared with that of humans and common mammalian pets, so they can become ill quickly, develop few symptoms, and die before a veterinarian can provide treatment. For this reason, your vet takes blood samples during the first exam to develop baseline measurements for the bird's blood chemistry. The measurements from the complete blood count (often called a CBC) give the veterinarian an idea of how your cockatiel's body works when he is healthy, and having them on record will make it easier to quickly recognize problems that may occur later. The results of the first blood samples form an essential part of your cockatiel's permanent medical history.

Blood tests also allow your veterinarian to detect whether your cockatiel is suffering from diabetes or has liver or kidney problems, which might not be obvious from a superficial exam. Blood tests can also detect certain types of cancers and a variety of dangerous illnesses, including pathogens with which the bird has had contact, even if he hasn't developed the disease itself. If a cockatiel is the carrier of certain diseases, he could spread the illnesses to other parrots just by being present in the same room, and sometimes the diseases could kill affected birds.

In addition to taking blood samples, the veterinarian conducts a complete physical. This includes checking your cockatiel's eyes, mouth, cere, legs, toes, wings, and general feather texture and development. The vet palpates the throat and crop for possible tumors or impactions of the crop. The area of the vent is scanned carefully for any signs of diarrhea, swelling, or bleeding, and the uropygial gland over the base of the tail is checked as well (because tumors of this gland are not uncommon in parrots). The veterinarian weighs your bird and takes note of how much fat is present under the skin of the chest. Excess fat may be an indication of a poor diet, lack of exercise, or possibly a more serious problem. The adult cockatiel's weight should stay approximately the same throughout his life, and it's important to have this baseline measurement to guard against obesity. Obesity is a common problem in cockatiels and can lead to a number of diseases.

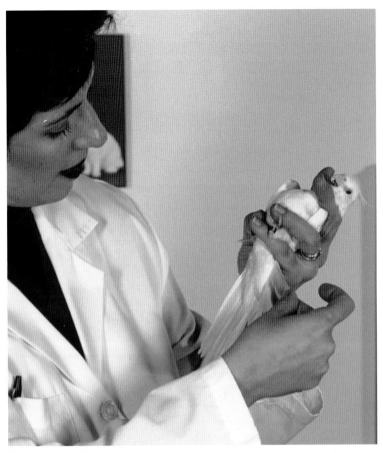

Take your cockatiel to the vet as soon as possible after you purchase him, and schedule yearly examinations thereafter.

At this first visit, the veterinarian may take a fecal sample and check it for parasites. Giardia is one of the more common intestinal parasites in pet birds, and this single-celled organism can cause diarrhea, weight loss, lethargy, and feather picking. Some infected birds show no symptoms, but your veterinarian may want to test for it if the illness (called giardiasis) is common in your part of the country. The usual treatment is an antibiotic or an antiprotozoal medication.

Your veterinarian may ask whether you want to have a DNA test performed on your bird. This blood test allows you to learn your bird's sex (it is difficult to tell the sex of some color mutations), and it can identify certain potentially fatal diseases.

Stay Calm

FEW VETERINARIANS LIKE TO EXAMINE A SCREAMING bird, and they certainly don't like being bitten. You are responsible for making sure that your new pet is calm enough to handle. If he isn't already, your bird certainly should be towel trained by the next annual exam. (See chapter 5 for towel training.) A veterinarian may anesthetize a bird for an examination, but rarely. Although several safe anesthetics are available, anesthesia is always considered a danger for a small animal and is used only when necessary (such as with surgery or with treating a severe injury). Towel training your bird is much safer.

Annual Visits

Plan to take your cockatiel to the veterinarian for a checkup each year, with a full blood workup every three years to keep your bird's blood chemistry records accurate (chemistry can change with age). During the annual checkup, the veterinarian performs the usual external examination, paying special attention to the eyes, ears, cere, beak, toes, nails, chest, cloaca, wings, and feathers. The bird is weighed and his current weight compared with past weights to help ensure he is on the proper diet. You may also ask the veterinarian to trim your cockatiel's wing feathers and nails while you are there.

Depending on where you live and the number of tests and grooming services the veterinarian performs, an initial visit and

Many cockatiels are easy to handle and don't require restraint, but any bird may object to being handled when sick and frightened. Your vet will appreciate it if you've towel trained your pet.

annual checkups may cost from one hundred to three hundred dollars—which may be more than the cost of the cockatiel. Remember that a young cockatiel can look forward to ten to twenty years or more in your care if given a healthy diet and regular veterinary care. Do all you can to ensure that your bird has a long and healthy life.

Emergencies

In nature, a sick bird is the first to be noticed by a predator and then picked off. For this reason, birds often show no signs of illness until their final days, or hours, are near. This is why annual veterinary visits, including lab tests, are important for your cockatiel. You need to keep a close eye on your bird's behavior and appearance and note any changes, no matter how small. If your bird becomes quieter or noisier than usual, is more or less affectionate, ignores a favorite toy or snack, or stops drinking, consult your veterinarian immediately. There may be nothing wrong (though failure to drink is usually a sign of a serious problem), but it is better to make a phone call and at least talk to the veterinarian than let a serious problem develop. Many illnesses can be fatal in one or two days from the time obvious signs first appear.

For minor respiratory problems, you can take temporary measures the moment you notice sneezing or a runny nostril. Keep your bird warm and reduce his activity by moving him to a smaller cage with just one perch low off the floor. Use a lightbulb or heating pad (over the cage, never in it) to keep the temperature at 90 degrees Fahrenheit, and make sure the cage isn't in a draft. When you take the bird to the veterinarian, take him in his smaller travel cage, and perhaps place a hand towel in the cage to help him stay warm.

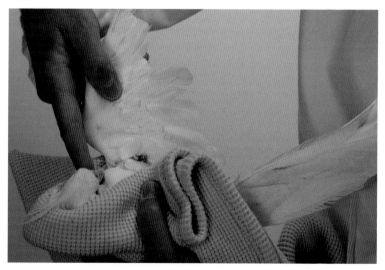

Like most prey animals, cockatiels may mask signs of illness until a serious medical problem has already developed. As soon as you suspect a problem, call your veterinarian, or take your bird in for an evaluation.

Bleeding is probably the most common medical emergency for cockatiels (and parrots in general), and blood loss can rapidly become fatal. An actively growing blood feather—one that is just forming (see "Trimming Wing Feathers" below)—may break, or the bird may catch a toenail in the cage bars or on a toy and pull off a nail. If not treated, both problems can lead to serious blood loss, so they require veterinary attention. You can slow down most bleeding (if it's not from a flesh wound) by applying a styptic powder (sold in pet stores and veterinary offices) or with liberal applications of cornstarch or flour to absorb the blood and help it clot; then head for the vet immediately.

Trimming Wing Feathers

Trimming the wing feathers of your cockatiel is one of the most important steps you can take to keep your bird safe. Cockatiels startle easily, which can trigger sudden, haphazard flight—straight into a window, wall, or mirror; up to a high point out of your reach; or even right out the door. This is why it is important to keep their wing feathers trimmed at all times. Cockatiels with both wings trimmed correctly are able to jump a couple of feet as well as glide down safely from a high point such as your shoulder or the top of the cage. A wing-trimmed bird is also easier to tame.

Trimming your cockatiel's wing feathers is just like cutting your own hair. No bones or muscles are cut—just feathers, which grow back. And because they grow back with each molt, which happens about twice a year, trimming is a grooming chore you'll want to be able to do yourself. Have a veterinarian or bird breeder show you how to do it the first time so you know which feathers to cut and which to avoid. You should never trim a blood feather; blood feathers are new feathers just starting to

Cockatiels who are allowed to be loose in the house should have their wing feathers trimmed. Have your veterinarian trim both wings regularly, or ask to be shown how to do it yourself.

emerge from their protective sheaths under the skin of the wing. They are liberally supplied with blood during this stage of growth, and cutting them could lead to serious bleeding. Keep styptic powder or cornstarch on hand in case you accidentally trim a blood feather, and be prepared to take your cockatiel to the veterinarian if the bleeding doesn't stop.

There are several ways to trim wing feathers, but the safest technique involves cutting just the first five to eight primary feathers—the long flight feathers. A strong cockatiel may need to have eight feathers cut, whereas a weaker cockatiel may need only five feathers trimmed. Start with five and let your bird take off from your hand about a foot off the floor. If the bird quickly gains altitude instead of gliding to the ground, trim one more feather on each side and try again. An ability to gain *some* altitude will prevent crash landings, but a cockatiel shouldn't be able to fly more than a couple of feet into the air.

In the past, some pet bird owners trimmed just one set of wing feathers, but this left the bird off balance and resulted in uneven flight and uncontrolled landings (and injury!). Trim the same number from both wings.

Keeping your cockatiel's wing feathers trimmed is a year-round job. The molt generally starts after the nesting season is over, when young birds would be out of the nest, but it occurs whether a cockatiel has bred or not. Generally, an old primary feather at about the middle of the wing is shed first, and then other primaries are shed in an alternating fashion on either side of the middle primary. Different types of parrots take different amounts of time to complete a molt, but cockatiels are relatively quick molters, usually molting twice a year over a period of six weeks for each molt. This is one reason many so-called trimmed cockatiels suddenly begin to fly in the late autumn and escape from owners who have not paid attention to the feather growth and neglected to trim them in time. Escaped cockatiels almost always die in a few days or weeks, so examine your bird's wing feathers regularly to keep your bird safe.

Trimming Nails

Nails should be trimmed on a regular basis—probably every two to three months. They may grow quickly, and a long nail is likely to be broken or become twisted, allowing it to be caught in the cage bars and your clothing. If the nail is pulled out, it can cause serious bleeding. Have your vet show you how to trim the nails; the process is not really difficult. You can use either a pair of nail clippers made for humans or the more complicated guillotine-type designed for cats. Both work well, but the simple type is easier to control. Cut only the very tips of the nails, which is dead tissue similar to your fingernails; never try to trim too far back, or you will cut into the live quick and cause bleeding.

Preventing Feather Picking

Parrots are intelligent birds who get bored easily, and they sometimes resort to plucking out their feathers out of boredom, much as you might bite your fingernails. Soon this activity becomes a

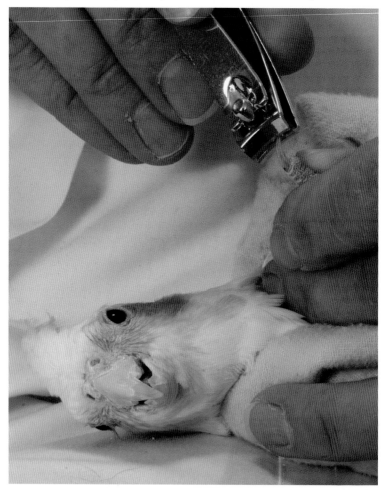

Your cockatiel's nails will grow quickly and will need to be trimmed regularly. You can save on veterinarian bills if you have your vet show you how to trim the nails at home.

Beak Trims

YOUR COCKATIEL'S BEAK SHOULDN'T NEED TRIMMING. *If it does, it can be a sign of an underlying medical problem, such as poor nutrition or even a disease. Examining the beak is part of a normal vet examination. If the beak needs trimming, leave it to the vet. Never trim the beak yourself.*

compulsive habit, more and more time is spent picking, and the bird ends up virtually naked. Aside from being unsightly, picking often results in serious sores and bleeding. But boredom is rarely the reason a cockatiel plucks out or picks at his feathers. If a cockatiel is picking at his feathers and skin, he may be suffering from an infection, a disease, or a nutritional deficiency. Your veterinarian can help you determine any underlying medical problems.

Although cockatiels aren't notorious feather pickers, keep your cockatiel active and exercised, as well as healthy. Interact with the bird several times a day, never place him in too small a cage, and give him lots of toys to keep him busy. Spending time on a playgym near his human companions often helps keep a cockatiel too busy to even think of picking. Giving your bird a companion might seem a good idea, but if the cause of the picking is a disease, the other cockatiel will become infected. And the two cockatiels may begin to pick each other!

A Healthy Bird's the Best

There are several very dangerous and deadly parrot diseases, but the likelihood of your captive-bred bird catching them is pretty rare, especially if you take certain precautions. Some diseases can

This poor fellow has had most of the feathers from his head and neck picked by a cage mate. Although many parrot species pick out of boredom, picking in cockatiels is more likely caused by underlying medical problems.

be picked up in a pet store or by visiting another bird, can be passed by a pigeon or sparrow flying over an outdoor cage, or can even be caught by going to a pet bird show. Taking your bird for regular visits to your veterinarian will help detect such diseases before they progress too far.

Newcastle Disease

Known also as avian pneumoencephalitis, Newcastle is a deadly, contagious disease. Caused by a virus, paramyxovirus-1, its first symptoms are sneezing and coughing; next are difficulties holding the wings and tail correctly, inability to walk, and strange head postures. Diarrhea and complete paralysis may follow, leading to death. Newcastle disease can spread through flocks of chickens and other poultry at a rapid rate, causing thousands to millions of dollars in losses of adult birds, chicks, and developing eggs in just a week. Losses of entire flocks are not uncommon, and the standard containment measure is to kill all poultry who might be infected or might be carrying the disease. Unfortunately, parrots (and feral pigeons) are excellent carriers of Newcastle.

Because this is such an economically significant disease, most states regularly check chicken flocks. They also require that birds (including parrots) entering the state be quarantined if they don't carry health certificates indicating they aren't carriers. Parrots of many types have been carriers of the disease in the past (and continue to be so), and in some parts of the country veterinarians are under governmental orders to keep an eye out for Newcastle. Although this disease is preventable through vaccinations, the low cost of a cockatiel and the low chance that a pet store cockatiel will carry Newcastle means that few are vaccinated.

Proventricular Dilatation Disease (PDD)

Proventricular dilatation disease (PDD), once called macaw wasting disease, is a serious and highly contagious viral disease that can infect cockatiels. With this disease, the proventriculus— the tube between the crop and the ventriculus (gizzard)— becomes inflamed, and nondigested food passes through, resulting in weight loss and poor muscle tone in the flight muscles. Chicks often die, and those who have been successfully weaned sometimes return to beg for food because they are not properly utilizing what they eat. Unfortunately, an infected bird may not develop signs of the disease for several years. The disease is not treatable, and diagnosis can be confirmed only by examining the ventriculus (and other organs) after the bird has died.

A cockatiel diagnosed with PDD can live for several years (sometimes almost a normal lifetime) if you keep him free of stress and feed him foods that are easy to digest or are already partially digested. Your vet will be able to give you a feeding regimen. Any bird known to be carrying PDD should not be allowed to come into contact with other birds.

Psittacosis, or Avian Chlamydiosis

Psittacosis was once called parrot fever but is now more properly called avian chlamydiosis (because it attacks many bird species, not just parrots). This contagious disease is caused by the bacterium *Chlamydophila psittaci* and is one of the few bird diseases that can be transferred to humans. In humans, the disease is typically known as psittacosis. From 1988 to 2003, 935 human cases were reported to the U.S. Centers for Disease Control and Prevention. Once a dangerous human disease, psittacosis is now easily treated with antibiotics.

Humans usually pick up the bacteria by breathing infected dust from pigeon feces in old buildings and near park statues, not from a parrot. In humans, psittacosis symptoms generally include a fever and chills that could progress to pneumonia and death if left untreated. Commonly, the heart muscles and liver become inflamed, leading to long-term health problems.

Your cockatiel could catch this disease if he is regularly kept outdoors in a cage where droppings from infected pigeons and house sparrows could contaminate his food and water. Another source of infection is smuggled parrots from Mexico, who enter the pet trade without going through quarantine and can infect healthy cockatiels in the pet store. Your cockatiel can also contract psittacosis by being exposed to another pet bird with the disease. Psittacosis has few consistent signs in parrots other than bright lime-green droppings. It is detected most reliably by chemical and DNA tests of blood samples and treated with a course of antibiotics. Unfortunately, an infected parrot does not gain immunity and can come down with the disease again.

Giardiasis

Giardiasis is a disease caused by the protozoan genus *Giardia*, which contains several species of intestinal parasites that are common contaminants of food and water everywhere. In humans and most domestic mammals, minor *Giardia* infections cause diarrhea and nausea that soon pass with no serious problems, although children occasionally die from serious infections. In adult cockatiels, the primary symptom of a *Giardia* infection is feather picking under the wings and at the top of the legs, as if

You owe it to your companion to protect him from disease as much as possible. You'll have many years together to enjoy each other's company.

the bird has itchy skin. Other symptoms include weight loss and diarrhea. Unfortunately, one species, *Giardia psittaci*, can be fatal in young cockatiels.

The protozoan is spread through cysts in water and feces that have come into contact with other infected parrots, including the parents. Infected young cockatiels cannot properly digest their food; they eat heavily but lose weight, pick their feathers, scream, and are obviously uncomfortable. Eventually they die. If detected early through blood work and other tests, giardiasis can be treated by a knowledgeable veterinarian.

Avian Polyomavirus

Avian polyomavirus is highly infectious and is transferred among parrots (all species) through feather dust, through the feces, and through food fed to chicks by infected adults. Formerly called budgerigar fledgling disease, avian polyomavirus kills nestling and weaning parrots; older birds become carriers who show no symptoms of the disease. Infected birds may stop eating, develop hemorrhages under the skin, regurgitate, develop tremors, and die. There is no cure. The disease is not as common in cockatiels as it is in budgies, but you wouldn't want to knowingly expose a carrier to your bird. To detect the disease, a veterinarian may take a cloacal swab or a blood test: if the virus is detected, the bird definitely has the disease; but the bird may still have the disease even if the virus does not appear to be present.

Pacheco's Disease

Like polyomavirus, Pacheco's is a highly contagious disease that could potentially be controlled by a vaccine. Some birds have shown negative reactions to the vaccine, so your veterinarian may advise against it; the relatively few instances of Pacheco's in cockatiels may not warrant the risk. As with polyomavirus, prevention is the best defense. The disease is spread through sneezing, nasal discharge, and feces, so keep your pet away from infected birds. There are few obvious external symptoms (such as diarrhea, ruffled feathers, and lethargy) of the disease, so birds who seem healthy may suddenly appear ill. The disease can be detected through blood tests.

Common Infections

Cockatiels are also susceptible to a variety of infections. Bacterial and fungal infections are fairly common in cockatiels, and they can be hard to detect. Some signs of bacterial infections are listlessness or a change in behavior, but a lab test is required for diagnosis. Some birds show no signs at all, so regular veterinary exams are crucial.

Yeast infections are also common in cockatiels, especially in young chicks (whose immune systems aren't highly developed) and in birds that have been on antibiotics. Yeast infections can also result from vitamin A deficiency or from ingesting rotting food. In cockatiels, the infection usually involves the digestive tract but may also affect the intestines. Signs of yeast infections are white cheeselike lesions in the mouth with a sticky residue, a thickened crop, and diarrhea. Again, there may not be any visible signs of infection, so the condition won't be detected until a vet examines the bird. Luckily, yeast infections are easily treatable if detected early in otherwise healthy birds.

7

Cockatiel Breeding Basics

These little nestlings can melt your heart, and breeding your own cockatiels can be very rewarding. Unless you're a dedicated breeder who intends to breed birds for show, make sure you have homes for your newcomers before you let your cockatiels mate.

Cockatiels breed easily and often, and pairs form quickly and are relatively permanent. There is little doubt that if you have a male and female of the right age and in good health, you can successfully breed your pets. Whether you *should* breed them is a matter to be considered first.

Should You Breed Your Cockatiels?

There are competitive cat shows, competitive dog shows, and even competitive bird shows. For many pet owners, the ability to produce an ideal representation of a particular breed or species is a point of pride. For others, the practice of competitive showing—and the hobby breeding it requires—creates cause for concern. What happens to the less-than-perfect birds? Or the birds for whom a breeder cannot find homes? Who will care for them all? Once, this was not an ethical or practical problem for bird breeders, as most pet bird species were in low supply and few pet stores carried birds other than the traditional canaries, finches, and budgies. This is no longer true, and a real question exists as to what you will do with the young your birds produce.

Commercial Breeding

Parrots, especially budgies and cockatiels, are bred commercially by hundreds of breeders all over the country. Pet superstores carry thousands of pet birds. Smaller breeders sell over the Internet, and many local pet stores buy from larger, well-established bird breeders who supply stores with their entire live inventory. The odds are good that if you start breeding cockatiels, you will not be able to sell them to any local pet stores.

If you sell your birds, you may be required to obtain permits from local, state, and even federal agencies (if you cross state lines in your sales). Such permits may require inspection of your breeding facilities and detailed reports of all your transactions. You also may have to register as a business and file special tax statements. Breeding cockatiels—or any other birds—for sale can be a very complicated business. And it is a business, not just a casual hobby.

Hobby Breeding

If you want to be a hobby breeder and plan to place the birds with people you know (such as friends, relatives, and co-workers with interests in birds), then you are on much firmer ground, and there really is no reason for you not to try your hand at a clutch or two. Never assume that you have enough interested friends to take

For hobby breeding, you'll need a nest box similar to this one where your birds can lay their eggs and brood them.

Age Requirements

ALTHOUGH MALE COCKATIELS BEGIN TO DEVELOP THEIR full adult coloration and behaviors at six months, they are not fully mature until at least a year old; females mature a bit more slowly. You can successfully breed birds who are just a year old, but it is generally better for the birds and their offspring if you wait until they are eighteen months old. Very young birds often don't know how to take care of their eggs or feed their young.

your surplus, however. You will probably want to keep one or two young each year as pets and as replacements for the birds you lose through accidents, illness, or age. But what do you do with the rest? Cockatiels can be very prolific breeders, and it isn't ethical to produce an overpopulation that may end up in animal shelters.

This is a healthy pair, ready for breeding.

It is also important to consider the commitment of money and time that will be required to breed your cockatiels successfully. Breeding can be expensive, especially when you factor in veterinary costs. And if you hand-rear one or more fledglings to produce strongly human-bonded pets, expect to spend more than a month feeding chicks several times a day.

Sexing

Most parrots are *monomorphic*, meaning that the sexes look virtually identical. Fortunately, cockatiels are *dimorphic*—adult males have color and pattern characteristics that differ from the females'. For a normal gray cockatiel, the differences are obvious (see chapter 1). In many color varieties, the differences are harder to

Technical Sexing

SO HOW DO DNA TESTS DETERMINE THE SEX OF BIRDS?

Male parrots have two large sex chromosomes termed XX, whereas females have one large X chromosome and one small Y chromosome. Only a female carries a Y, so in theory the female determines sex of the offspring. (This is roughly the opposite of the situation in mammals, where males carry the small sex chromosome. It is also the reason most geneticists use the letters Z and W for birds and X and Y for mammals, to prevent confusion.) Today, it is possible to determine the sex of monomorphic birds by analyzing the DNA content of blood samples, a process known as DNA sequencing. Several companies perform DNA analyses at reasonable prices and with quick turnaround times.

For many years, veterinarians determined the sex of birds by performing a surgical procedure known as laparoscopy, which allowed them to view the sex organs. Laparoscopies are now considered unreliable by some breeders and may not work at all on young birds.

see, but as a rule, females have duller faces than males do and retain at least traces of barring on the tail feathers and spotting under the wings. With experience, you can visually determine the sex of most birds who are more than six months old. Unfortunately, pieds, lutinos, and other varieties who are largely white cannot be sexed reliably just by external appearance, unless they happen to show some barring on the tail or wing feathers, indicating they are females. (See chapter 8 for more on color varieties.) For these birds, you will need a DNA blood test to determine the sex.

The Breeding Process

Start with a pair of healthy cockatiels of breeding age—preferably eighteen months or older. If both are pets and tightly bonded to you (especially the female), the birds may not want to pay much attention to each other at first. Put them in separate cages where they can hear each other to try to increase their interest. You will probably have to reduce your playtime with the birds as well, as you want them to become birds again rather than pets—for at least a while. One disadvantage of breeding pet cockatiels is that they become protective and territorial during nesting; but their sweet pet nature usually returns once breeding and caring for the chicks is complete.

After a week or two, place the birds together in a large cage—the larger the better—with at least one nest box hanging in a far corner. The nest box should simulate a natural nest hole in a rotting tree—about ten inches square at the bottom, a foot high, and with an entrance hole roughly three and one-half inches in diameter just below the top on one side. Place a handful of pine shavings in the bottom for cushioning the eggs, and place a perch under the entrance hole if needed. Nest boxes

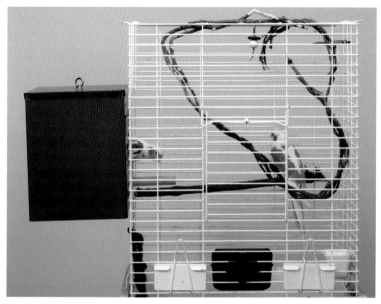

When your birds are ready to mate, put them together in a breeding cage with a nesting box attached, as shown here.

If you're lucky, you may observe your pair mating.

for cockatiels are widely sold in pet stores and by mail and come in many styles and materials, so finding one for your cockatiels shouldn't be much of a problem.

Cockatiels mate frequently, with each mating being accomplished very swiftly. It is also not unusual for matings to continue for two weeks before the first egg is laid.

Nesting

Cockatiel eggs are white, about an inch long and three-fourths of an inch in diameter. Clutches average four to seven eggs that are laid over a period of time rather than all at once; the female typically lays an egg every two days. Incubation starts when the first egg is laid, so the eggs hatch at different times. Average incubation periods in cockatiels are nineteen to twenty-one days, which means that the first young to hatch from a large clutch will be much larger and better developed (having been fed for several days) when the last egg hatches. In nature, it is likely that the last one or two young to hatch don't receive sufficient food and die, but you can make sure that the parents are well fed and can keep their chicks happy.

Egg Binding

If an egg cannot leave the female's cloaca, the bird is said to be egg bound. This is not an uncommon condition with very young and very old cockatiels or with those who are bred when not in excellent health. Often, egg binding results simply from a lack of sufficient muscle tone that prevents the egg from being forced out of the oviduct. Or, if the diet is lacking in minerals and calcium, the hen's system may be unable to form thick shells around the eggs, preventing them from passing through the

Your cockatiels will brood the eggs for about twenty days.

oviduct. Even a healthy bird may become egg bound if she becomes sick while laying. An egg-bound bird quickly becomes dull, sits fluffed in a corner, does not eat or drink, and can die in a few days. It is important to know that cockatiels will lay eggs even when not mated, so a female who is housed alone can also become egg bound.

Sometimes immersing the hen in warm water will help her expel the stuck egg; keep her warm with an ambient temperature of 90 degrees Fahrenheit (such as in a small bathroom with a hot shower running). This method will not work on shell-less eggs, of course, and it is always best to call your veterinarian immediately whenever you think your bird is egg bound. Injections of calcium compounds and hormones or even surgery may be required to relieve your bird.

The Nestlings

Cockatiel chicks have coats of yellow or white down over their bodies and are kept warm by the parents, by their siblings, and by the remaining unhatched eggs. Chicks cannot maintain their own body temperatures for at least a week, so they are subject to death from chills, damp nest boxes, and drafts. The mother and father take turns feeding the chicks partially digested seeds and pellets, and the chicks grow quickly. They are fed by the parents for about four to five weeks before they leave the nest and start feeding on their own. They will continue to beg for food from their parents (or from you!) for several weeks; this is the perfect time to start bonding with a young bird. Some breeders prefer to remove the chicks from the parents to hand-feed them through the entire nestling and weanling stages to help them become well-adjusted, human-bonded pets.

If you want to hasten the bonding process, remove chicks from their parents at this nestling age and hand-feed them yourself.

Raising Your Own Cockatiels

Sometimes the parent cockatiels have to be removed from the nest—perhaps they become ill or the weather becomes so cold that you have to incubate the eggs yourself and then hand-feed the young. Hatching out eggs is not a problem, but hand-feeding is extremely time consuming and requires special techniques to feed the chicks safely. For these reasons, most home breeders just leave the eggs with their parents. Sometimes it may be necessary to try to foster the eggs or young to another pair of cockatiels who also are nesting. Cockatiels make good parents and usually will accept some strange eggs and young.

Sanitation

BIRDS ARE MESSY, AS WE ALL KNOW, AND THE NEST BOX *will be quite dirty at the end of the nesting period. Although females may move some feces to one side of the box to keep the nestlings relatively clean, you will have to take apart the box and sanitize it completely when the fledglings have left. Some nest boxes are disposable and can just be thrown away after the season is over. Be aware that many females lay a second clutch while still feeding the first clutch, so you may have to wait for months to clean the box.*

Hatching

You'll need an incubator to successfully hatch cockatiel eggs. Incubators are designed to provide a constant temperature the entire time the eggs are developing. Incubators consist of a heating element, an accurate thermometer, and a cup area for the eggs.

Eggs do not have to be kept at incubation temperatures (near 100 degrees Fahrenheit) for the first three to five days after they are laid if they are kept at temperatures in the 50 to 60 degrees Fahrenheit range; so you can collect eggs as they are laid, place them carefully in a layer of tissue paper, and hold them in a warm spot until you have enough eggs to put in the incubator. Eggs that aren't incubated more than five days probably won't hatch, and those cooled to 45 degrees Fahrenheit or less certainly won't.

All but the most expensive incubators won't have a means for turning the eggs, so you have to turn them manually. Bird eggs must be turned at least three or five times a day (the parents may turn the eggs fifteen to twenty times) at fairly regular intervals; this prevents the embryo's body from sticking

This is a typical hobbyist's incubator for hatching eggs.

to the membranes on one side of the egg and either dying or becoming deformed. When you remove an egg from the nest box, use a soft pencil to mark the top with the date. (Some

Candling

***I**F YOU ARE INCUBATING THE EGGS, YOU PROBABLY WANT* *to make sure they are fertile before spending too much time on them; candling devices can help. Candlers may be simple or expensive, but basically they are very bright pinpoint sources of light directed through the shell of an egg to show whether growth is occurring inside the egg. Once an egg has begun incubation, the embryo begins to grow and form organs, including blood vessels along the inside of the shell. These are visible by the third day, appearing as a web of fine lines in the shell. In later days, the embryo grows larger and more of the egg becomes opaque; an infertile egg remains translucent.*

breeders believe the chemicals in a felt-tip marker may be toxic.) This way you not only will know the age of the egg (remember: nineteen to twenty-one days of incubation) but also will have one clearly marked surface to track your turning. Turn the eggs an uneven number of times each day, being sure to keep track of the turns: you don't want an egg to spend two nights with the same side down.

Assuming everything goes smoothly—and it usually does with cockatiels—in about three weeks you will have a group of nestling cockatiels to take care of. Move them to a brooder where they are kept warm (95 to 98 degrees Fahrenheit) for their first two weeks: remember that they cannot hold their own body temperatures yet. Later, you can move them to progressively cooler brooders as they become able to regulate their body temperatures.

Hand-Feeding

Next is the difficult part: getting the chicks to feed and grow until they are on their own. There are too many details to hand-feeding baby cockatiels to cover here, so look for a book on the subject, talk to an experienced breeder, or get some advice and instruction from your veterinarian. No two breeders do everything exactly the same way, so you have some leeway in how to feed the babies. Regardless of method, the object is to provide the chicks with enough food of the right temperature so they always have a full (not overfull) crop, all the while keeping them warm and clean.

Cockatiel chicks should be fed every two or three hours during the day over a roughly fourteen-hour period; that translates to a lot of work on your part. You cannot deviate from the

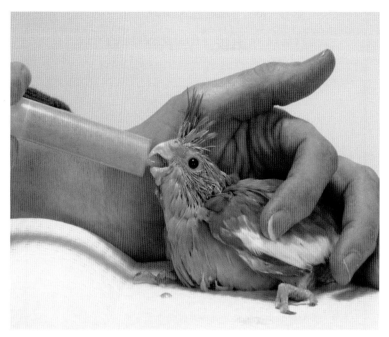

This chick is being hand-fed with a syringe—a very time-intensive procedure. Luckily, you won't have to feed them during the night!

schedule, as the little birds do not have enough resources to miss even one meal if you are away. Fortunately, you do not have to feed the birds at night because their parents don't either.

Most breeders use commercial hand-feeding formulas from a specialty pet store or an Internet-based supplier. The food must contain all the nutrients a growing chick needs—in the right amounts and in a form that is easy to dispense and digest. Breeders once made up their own rearing foods, varying from oatmeal mixes to milk mixed with monkey chow and peanut butter, but often with unexpected results and poor success rates. Stick to commercial hand-feeding formulas.

The basic feeding technique consists of inserting a small syringe (without a needle) filled with food into the gape at the

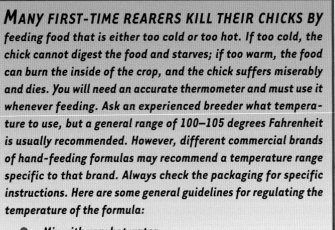

Watch the Temperature!

MANY FIRST-TIME REARERS KILL THEIR CHICKS BY *feeding food that is either too cold or too hot. If too cold, the chick cannot digest the food and starves; if too warm, the food can burn the inside of the crop, and the chick suffers miserably and dies. You will need an accurate thermometer and must use it whenever feeding. Ask an experienced breeder what tempera-ture to use, but a general range of 100–105 degrees Fahrenheit is usually recommended. However, different commercial brands of hand-feeding formulas may recommend a temperature range specific to that brand. Always check the packaging for specific instructions. Here are some general guidelines for regulating the temperature of the formula:*

- *Mix with very hot water*
- *Cool to the recommended temperature*
- *Stir to make sure there are no hot spots*
- *Use an accurate thermometer at each stage*
- *Do not let the temperature go below 100 degrees*

back of the right side of the beak (the right side as you face the bird, which is actually the bird's left side). Some breeders report that feeding from the left side can allow food into the lungs, which ultimately causes death. For a young nestling, give about two cc's of formula at a feeding. You will see that the chick starts to gulp down the mix as soon as the first bits touch the tongue. You want the crop to become full but not grossly inflated, so carefully palpate the crop during feeding, and judge the amount to be given by the condition of the crop. Older birds will require considerably more formula, which you can give through a tea-spoon crimped at the end to form a narrow channel.

These adorable weanlings are ready to begin switching to an adult diet. You must make this change gradually, still providing a lot of soft foods while introducing easy-to-digest pellets to their diets.

Weaning

It takes about five weeks for chicks to reach their maximum weight. At this stage, the cockatiel's crop is still relatively large and lacks feathering along the center and up toward the throat. Now you feed fewer times a day, but you still should not miss regular feedings. Your veterinarian or an experienced breeder should be able to give you details of what to expect. The chicks should now be feathered and flexing their wings, hopping out of the brooder box and trying to cozy up to you for food and companionship. They are now fledglings, a stage that may last two or three weeks in most cockatiels. It's about time to think of trimming the wing feathers (see chapter 6) as the chicks will now learn to take flight. Trimming wing feathers gradually, such as trimming just one primary wing feather on both sides each week, will allow your cockatiel to learn how to land and maneuver during the fledgling stage.

Feeding Fledglings

Fledglings eat a more adult food mix, but they still need some rearing food as they gradually switch from feeding the way nestlings do to feeding the way adults do. Remember that parent cockatiels feed their chicks from their crops, so you will need to supply the fledglings with plenty of soft, nutritious foods. Don't just suddenly switch completely to adult foods—this could kill the young birds. Instead, add more and more solid food (pelleted foods are best because they are easier to digest, and they are the bulk of the adult diet anyway) with some tidbits of Cheerios, cooked carrot or yam, scrambled egg, cooked oatmeal, or cooked warm rice.

After your fledglings have been successfully weaned onto an adult pelleted diet, you can feed them an occasional treat.

A millet spray will draw the attention of young birds, and they will quickly learn to eat this adult food.

8

Cockatiel Color
Variations

You won't find mutations like these in the wild, but they have been carefully bred in cockatiels for years.

Because cockatiels are bred in such large numbers and have been widely bred for about a century, it was only a matter of time until they began to produce colors that varied from the norm. Such variations are called *mutations*, and they are responsible for the interestingly colored cockatiels seen in some pet stores and featured at cockatiel shows.

Mutations

Chromosomes carry genes, which are specific combinations of a few amino acids that form complex chemical chains known as DNA. The different combinations of amino acids tell a cell when to produce certain other chemicals, such as proteins and enzymes, in the developing embryo or when to turn specific growth activities on and off. The differences between species and individuals are largely due to very small differences in the chemistry of the genes.

When an outside energy source destroys or rearranges portions of a chromosome, deleting or modifying genes, a mutation results. Mutations are inherited: any offspring will carry the modified genes. Most mutations are neutral, having little or no effect on whether an organism survives and can reproduce. Many mutations are harmful or deadly, causing a change that prevents an embryo from developing completely or normally. Very few mutations are good in the sense that they give an organism a slight advantage over others of its species, allowing it to interact better with the environment and produce more offspring that carry the special gene. Here are two examples of good mutations: birds found in warm, dry areas have developed pale coloration that absorbs little light and reduces the need to rid the body of excess heat; those from cold, humid areas often have darker

Here are examples of a light and a dark coloration in cockatiels.

feathers that absorb more heat from the sun and surroundings and keep the bird warm.

To a breeding or showing enthusiast, a good mutation is one that affects the way the colors of a cockatiel are formed and inherited. Color mutations can be carefully bred to produce more and more of these special colors and patterns. In nature, such color variations would probably disappear quickly because they would make the birds stand out from the flock and attract more predators. Some color mutations, such as recessive silver, originally produced birds that were almost blind and had difficulty breeding. Fortunately, silvers can be bred and exist safely in a cage or aviary.

More than a dozen color mutations have been bred in cockatiels since the 1940s, but only a few are likely to be found in pet stores. Many are rare or very subtle and are likely to be

This is a beautiful cinnamon pearl whiteface mutation.

seen only at larger bird shows and cockatiel specialty shows. This chapter will cover only the most common color mutations—the ones likely to be seen by new bird owners. Cockatiel color genetics is very complicated, as you might imagine, and entire books have been written on how to predict the results of many different matings. If you are genetically inclined or just curious, you might take a look at the cockatiel genetics section of the North American Cockatiel Society Web site at http://www.cockatiel.org/genetics. There you will find charts and explanations for almost any cross you could imagine, including rare mutations.

Common Cockatiel Color Mutations

Compared with some parrots, cockatiels have a very limited number of color possibilities. These consist mainly of grays produced by melanin pigments, which can be diluted into browns of varying tones; and yellows and reds caused by xanthin and erythrin pigments, respectively. The yellows and reds are commonly called *carotenoid colors*, and their intensity can be increased or decreased with diet without altering their genetics. If all these pigments are absent, the bird is white. Different genes generally affect how pigments are deposited in the feathers—their intensity, their pattern, and even when they develop or disappear during the life of a bird. No single gene controls all the variations in color in cockatiels.

As noted in chapter 1, cockatoos and cockatiels lack blue coloration. The appearance of blue feathering is not created by a pigment but by the structure of the feather itself and the way it reacts to light. When this type of feather has an overlying layer of yellow pigment, the feather appears green. Because cockatiels

Although not as colorful as many parrots, cockatiels have developed many beautiful color mutations, such as this gorgeous pearl.

lack both blue and green colors (called *structural colors*), they cannot be produced by any mutation.

The following are just some of the more familiar mutations of cockatiels likely to be encountered. Not all mutations are easy to recognize unless you have experience with cockatiel colors.

Lutino

First known to have appeared about fifty years ago, the lutino mutation produces white or creamy yellow cockatiels with bright face colors. The mutation prevents melanin (the gray pigment) from being formed or deposited in the feathers, so normally gray areas (such as the back, belly, wings, tail, beak, nails) have no dark pigment. When gray is removed from the face and crest, the yellow and red pigments are allowed to show in their full glory, so even females have bright yellow faces and deep orange ear patches. Females usually can be distinguished from males by traces of barring (yellow on white) under the wings and tail, but some birds are very difficult to sex visually. The eyes are red (no black in the iris) but look darker as the bird matures, and the beak and nails are pinkish.

Lutino is a sex-linked recessive mutation, so when you mate a normal gray male with a lutino female, all the young are phenotypically gray, with the males carrying the lutino gene hidden by the dominant gray. When you cross a lutino male with a normal gray female (females cannot be split in any sex-linked mutation), on the other hand, the female offspring are lutinos but the males are still splits. When both parents are lutinos, the offspring are lutinos. One fault of most lutinos is a bald area behind the crest; birds with the smallest possible featherless area are much preferred.

Genetics-Speak

GENETICISTS HAVE DEVELOPED A VERY COMPLICATED and detailed terminology to explain how traits are inherited, but fortunately few of these terms are needed for discussions of basic mutations. You should be aware of at least the following terms:

● *Genotype: the genetic makeup of an organism, literally the distribution of different genes. Genotypes are hidden and cannot always be determined from the appearance of an organism.*

● *Phenotype: the external appearance of an organism, which does not always reflect its genotype. For instance, the same coloration can be caused by several different gene combinations yet appear identical externally.*

● *Dominant: a gene (and thus trait) that is "strong" and rules other corresponding genes.*

● *Recessive: a gene (and thus trait) that is overruled or hidden by another, dominant, gene.*

● *Allele: one of two different versions of a gene that occurs at the same location on a chromosome. Commonly one allele is dominant, one recessive.*

● *Sex-linked: said of a trait that is carried only on the group of genes that controls sex. The sex chromosome Y of the female never carries the trait and cannot overrule it, so any female carrying the trait on her X chromosome will display that color. Lutino, cinnamon, and pearl are commonly seen sex-linked mutations.*

● *Autosomal: said of a trait that is inherited through the nonsex chromosomes and not dependent on the sex of the bird. Many mutations, such as pied, silver, and whiteface, are autosomal recessive mutations.*

● *Homozygous: a situation in which both genes for a single trait are the same, either both dominant or both recessive.*

● *Split: heterozygous, with both a dominant and a recessive gene for a trait; dominant genes hide recessive genes, so if heterozygous for a trait, an organism displays the dominant trait and carries the recessive one.*

● *Letter notation: simple abbreviations used to represent different mutations by one or two letters. (Not all works and authorities use the same abbreviations for the same trait, which of course causes a great deal of confusion.)*

Lutinos have no gray pigment in their feathers. This pretty lutino is nearly white, with touches of yellow.

Clear Pied or Black-Eyed White

The clear pied is an autosomal recessive mutation (not sex-linked) that produces what at first glance looks like a very clean white lutino with a pale yellow face and crest and a pale orange ear patch. However, the eyes are black (deep brown) rather than red. This is just one of several examples of mutations in which cockatiels appear identical (phenotypically the same), or certainly very similar, but have a very different genetic makeup (genotypically different).

Pied

Pied is an autosomal recessive mutation that has been known since at least 1949 and is one of the most commonly sold mutation colors. A pied cockatiel has patches of normally gray feathers that lack melanin and thus appear white or (rarely) yellow. There may be either a few white feathers or irregular large white patches over most of the back and belly; it is very difficult to produce a pied with symmetrical patches. The pale blotches typically are larger in females than in males, and females lack barring under the tail, being virtually indistinguishable from males.

Crossing a pied with a pied results in all pied young, whereas crossing a normal gray with a pied (the sex of the specific parents does not matter) results in all normal-looking young who carry the pied gene—typical of breeding autosomal recessive mutations. Crossing these phenotypically normal gray offspring with each other or with mates of either normal gray (homozygous) or pied color results in a very complicated mix of pied and phenotypically normal gray birds who could be either homozygous or split. Split-pied cockatiels often have a marking at the nape of their necks and may have pied markings in their beaks or on their feet.

Pied cockatiels have patches of gray and white in a variety of different patterns.

Pearl

Originating in West Germany in 1967, pearl is externally similar to pied, with large patches of white (or pale yellow) over the bird's body wherever gray melanin pigments are suppressed. However, pearl is a sex-linked recessive mutation and is thus inherited, whereas pied is not. In a pearl cockatiel, the center of each feather is pale, so the edge of the feather is dark (entire feathers are pale in pieds), producing a pattern known as lacing or pearling. One oddity of this mutation is that young pearl males resemble females, but when they molt into the adult pattern at about six months of age, the lacing disappears. Thus, an adult male pearl cockatiel is externally almost identical to a normal gray cockatiel. Crossing a normal gray male with a pearl female produces all gray females and males that are phenotypically gray but carry the pearl gene.

This close-up view shows the beautiful patterning possible in pearl cockatiels.

Cinnamon

In cinnamons, the melanin is present but is reduced in density so the bird appears brown rather than gray. Yellow and orange tones are muted, and the eyes are brown (changing from red within a few days of hatching). Intensity of brown varies greatly in different lines of cinnamons, and some birds (especially males) may have gray shadowing on some wing feathers. Cinnamon birds kept outdoors and exposed to sunlight may develop a marbled patterning in their feathers.

This is another sex-linked recessive mutation, so breeding a normal gray male with a cinnamon female produces all normal gray females and males that are phenotypically normal gray but carry the cinnamon gene. Cinnamon has been bred into many other color mutation cockatiels, especially pied and pearl. It is not advisable to create cinnamon-lutino birds, however, because lutino masks cinnamon, meaning you won't be able to see the cinnamon mutation.

Fallow

The fallow mutation also acts on the melanin pigment in the feathers and changes them from gray to brown, as in cinnamons; but fallow is an autosomal recessive mutation, not sex-linked. Fallows are hatched with red eyes and keep this color into adulthood.

Whiteface

The whiteface mutation suppresses the yellow and red pigments, so the face appears white, lacking yellow and the orange ear patches; the crest also is white. The body color, however, remains a fairly normal gray tone often called charcoal. This is an autosomal recessive mutation, so as you would expect, when you cross a whitefaced cockatiel with a normal gray, all the offspring appear normal gray but carry the gene for whiteface; crossing these offspring with whiteface results in whiteface birds. Crossing whiteface with whiteface results in all whiteface birds.

Cinnamons can have subtle or more intense brown coloring.

Albino

To a geneticist, the word *albino* means a lack of dark pigmentation in an organism. Thus, an albino corn snake (a widely bred pet snake) lacks black and brown, but it still has yellow and red pigments. In cockatiel breeding, the word *albino* is used to indicate a lack of all pigments—not only melanins but also yellow and red pigments. So an albino cockatiel is entirely white with red eyes and pink beak and nails. These birds are produced and sold as albinos, but they are not true albinos to a geneticist.

What is sold as an albino cockatiel is actually the result of crossing a lutino with a whiteface, traits that are on separate genes. (In a true albino, the trait would be passed as a single gene.) The sex-linked lutino mutation is a gene that suppresses all dark pigment (melanins) in the feathers, eyes, beak, and nails. The whiteface mutation, which is autosomal, eliminates the yellow and red pigments. Both genes are present when you mate a male lutino with a female whiteface and then mate one of the male babies (which appear lutino, carrying whiteface) back to a female whiteface cockatiel. This produces a lutino-whiteface, the bird often sold as an albino cockatiel. Breeding this color is complicated and takes at least three generations, so it is expensive to produce—and to purchase.

Silver

Once rare, the silver type (actually two different mutations) of cockatiel is being seen more often today. Here the normal gray coloration is replaced by a somewhat metallic silvery gray shade that varies in intensity in different lines. Both mutations are autosomal recessives. In recessive silver, the birds have red eyes, and the young look much like the adults, who are very difficult to

Albino cockatiels are all white with red eyes, a pink beak, and pink nails.

No matter what the color, cockatiels are distinguished by their long and delicate crests.

sex. In dominant silver, the eyes are dark brown to black as in normal gray cockatiels, and young males look like normal grays until after their first molt. Yellow tones are often stronger in dominant silvers than in recessive silvers. Other silver mutations can occur, so it can become very confusing unless you are deeply involved in cockatiel genetics.

Remember that many or most of these color mutations can be combined to produce wildly different-looking birds whose genetic ancestry can only be guessed. Experienced breeders prefer birds that are not greatly different from others in their line. They breed birds who look as much like their parents as possible; breeders don't like strange birds who don't conform to the accepted and published standards of what a mutation should look like. Breeders exhibit their birds at shows guided by the national clubs and compete to produce cockatiels who follow the standards. Most of the color mutation cockatiels sold in pet stores are not close to the standards in colors and patterns, but this, of course, does not make them any less desirable as pets.

Appendix

Cockatiel Societies

Cockatiel societies can be found around the world, but there are three major groups in the United States: the American Cockatiel Society (ACS), the National Cockatiel Society (NCS), and the North American Cockatiel Society (NACS). The ACS and NCS are relatively old societies, whereas the NACS is less than a decade old. All three have Web sites, offering articles and background information on cockatiels and allowing you to communicate with others interested in these fascinating little parrots. The Australian National Cockatiel Society also has information on keeping and breeding cockatiels. Other parrot societies may be found at http://www.parrotpages.com or at http://www.upatsix.com. Be sure to visit the Animal Network at http://www.animalnetwork.com.

AMERICAN COCKATIEL SOCIETY
http://www.acstiels.com

NATIONAL COCKATIEL SOCIETY
http://www.cockatiels.org

NORTH AMERICAN COCKATIEL SOCIETY
http://www.cockatiel.org

AUSTRALIAN NATIONAL COCKATIEL SOCIETY
www.cockatielsociety.org.au

Parrot Rescue Groups

FOSTER PARROTS, LTD.
http://www.fosterparrots.com

THE GABRIEL FOUNDATION
http://www.thegabrielfoundation.org

NATIONAL PARROT RESCUE AND PRESERVATION
FOUNDATION
http://www.parrotfestival.org

PARROT RESCUE INC.
http://www.parrotrescue.org

Glossary

albino: in cockatiels, lacking pigmentation; an albino bird is all white with red eyes and pink beak and nails

blood feathers: new feathers just starting to emerge from their protective sheaths; these feathers have an active blood supply

bumblefoot: a swelling of the ball of the foot that may abscess

Cacatuidae: the name used by some scientists for the cockatoo family, as separate from the parrot family

cere: the area of soft skin that includes a parrot's nostrils, found above the base of the beak

cloaca: the common opening in a bird through which the feces, urine, sperm, and eggs all pass; also called the vent

Convention on International Trade in Endangered Species (CITES): an intergovernmental agreement that regulates the importation and exportation of wild animals and plants

dimorphic: having distinct forms; physical differentiation between the sexes

fallow: a non-sex-linked mutation that produces a brown coloring

fledge: to leave the nest and begin learning to fly

hypervitaminosis: a vitamin overdose

lutino: a sex-linked mutation that produces white bodies and brightly colored faces

molt: the process of gradually shedding and replacing the feathers

monomorphic: having the same form; no physical differentiation between the sexes

mutations: changes in chromosomes that result in permanent changes that are inherited by offspring, such as color variations in cockatiels

Nymphicus hollandicus: the cockatiel's genus and species names

pearl: a sex-linked mutation that produces both light and dark feathering: the center of each feather is pale, and the edge of the feather is dark

pied: a non-sex-linked mutation that produces large patches of white and gray

preen: to groom the feathers with the beak

Psittacidae: the parrot family

psittacosis: an avian disease, more properly called avian chlamydiosis, that can be transferred to humans uropygial gland (preen gland): the oil gland at the base of the tail with which birds groom their feathers

vent: the cloaca

wean: to reach the period of growth where the chick switches to an adult diet

zygodactylous: foot pattern that forms an X, with two toes in front and two in back

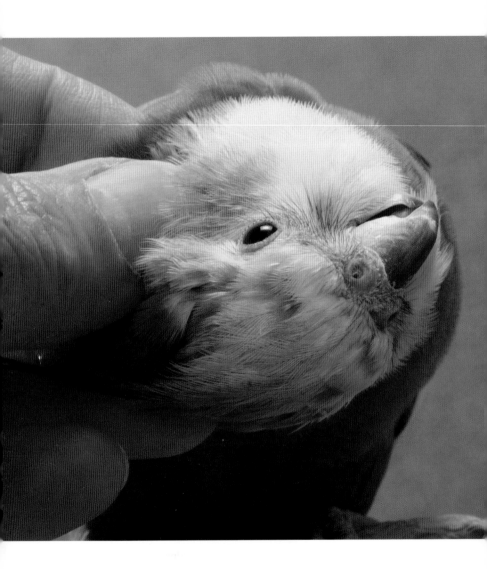

Index